The Unmumsy Mum

The UNMUMSY Mum

THE HILARIOUS HIGHS AND EMOTIONAL LOWS OF MOTHERHOOD

Sarah Turner

A TARCHERPERIGEE BOOK

An imprint of Penguin Random House LLC
375 Hudson Street
New York, New York 10014

Most TarcherPerigee books are available at special quantity discounts for bulk
purchase for sales promotions, premiums, fund-raising, and educational needs.
Special books or book excerpts also can be created to fit specific needs. For
details, write: SpecialMarkets@penguinrandomhouse.com.

Library of Congress Cataloging-in-Publication Data

Names: Turner, Sarah, 1987– author.
Title: The unmumsy mum: the hilarious highs and emotional
lows of motherhood / by Sarah Turner.
Description: New York: TarcherPerigee, [2017]
Identifiers: LCCN 2016040848 (print) | LCCN 2016056903 (ebook) |
ISBN 9780143130048 | ISBN 9781101993552
Subjects: LCSH: Motherhood. | Parenthood.
Classification: LCC HQ759 .T9435 2017 (print) |
LCC HQ759 (ebook) | DDC 306.874/3—dc23
LC record available at https://lccn.loc.gov/2016040848

Printed in the United States of America
1   3   5   7   9   10   8   6   4   2

BOOK DESIGN BY KATY RIEGEL

For Debbie Sheppard,

the greatest mum of all

(1954–2002)

Contents

Part Two: Life, but Not as We Knew It

Part Three: The Second Time Around

Part Four: The Daily Grind

Part Five: Cut Yourself Some Slack

Part Six: Wouldn't Change It for the World?

Meet the Turners

MOTHER 🐖 SARAH

aka The Unmumsy Mum

Writer/blogger/something or other. Has a first-class honors degree in philosophy (no, she hasn't ever "used" it). Drinks copious amounts of tea. Also partial to grown-up grape juice and G&Ts in tins. Unhealthily obsessed with the TV adaptation of *Wuthering Heights* (Tom Hardy as Heathcliff, proof dreams really can come true). Dicks around on Facebook a lot.

FIRSTBORN 🐖 HENRY

aka Henry Bear, Henners, H Bomb

Lover of Darth Vader, Scooby-Doo, and his Imaginary Monster Friend (called "Imaginary Monster Friend"). Forever guaranteed a card on Valentine's Day because it's his birthday. Enjoys conversing about farts and bums.

FATHER ☞ JAMES
aka Hubbs

Civil Servant Extraordinaire. Marathon watcher of car programs, marathon eater of biscuits, once ran a marathon (London, 2011), hated every second of it. Likes a kick around at the park. Hates being asked for "interesting facts" about himself. Switches place-name cards at weddings so his wife is next to the people they've never met. Would do anything for his family. An all-around Good Egg.

SECONDBORN ☞ JUDE
aka Jude Almighty, Ginger Biscuit, Judy Pops

If it's inedible, he'll eat it. If it's edible, he'll throw it. Treats the living room like an assault course. Rejected an array of beautiful "special bear" options presented in favor of Mummy Pig. A little Ron Weasley among a family of blonds.

About Mummy's Book:
A Letter to My Boys

Dearest Henry and Jude,

My wonderful boys, my Henry Bear and my Judy Pops.

If you are reading this, the chances are you are about to make your way through the rest of the book. I'm not sure how I feel about you delving into your mother's deepest thoughts from years gone by, but it was probably inevitable, so here we are.

First things first: I hope you are reading this as teenagers (and not before), because you will notice I occasionally use words I discourage you from using at home. I have always felt that writing down the words in my head, exactly as I think them, adds a certain authenticity to my writing, and it is unfortunate that, sometimes, the first word in my head is "cockwomble." Or "twat." These are still not appropriate words to call each other at home—you are never too old for that time-out chair.

Back when I was a teenager I wrote diaries. With a *pen and paper.* I'm aware that makes me sound ancient, and I guess I am ancient in your eyes. I was born in a different *millennium* to you two. I grew up in the 1990s, with the Spice Girls, Tamagotchis, hair mascara and taping the Top 40 off the radio (remind me to show you what tapes are). I'm not going to tell you what was in those diaries because, postschool years, they mainly detailed night-club flirting with your father (you can stop cringing; I burned them).

I stopped writing diaries soon after I met your dad, and it wasn't until I became a mum that I felt inspired to start jotting down my thoughts once more. Only this time, rather than writing in scented gel pens on carefully selected notepads from WHSmith (which I hid under my pillow), I started writing an online blog; and before I had really considered the implications of letting those thoughts loose on the world, they had already escaped my clutches. The Internet is scary like that.

So I would like to set a few things straight. Right here, right now. Not because I have to, but because I want you to understand why I have written so openly about being your mummy. I need you to understand what was going on in my head at the time, because you two, my little pudding heads, have always been at the very heart of it.

Being a mummy is really hard.

Whatever age you are when you read this, I have no doubt I will still be finding motherhood hard, but those early years were something else. On the darkest of sleep-deprived days—when one of you was screaming, I was irritable and the house looked like a war zone—I wanted to read about somebody who was having a dark day, too. Somebody who would reassure me I wasn't going completely mad. Somebody who would tell me there was no need to poke my own eyes out in despair because it would all be okay (but that, in the meantime, it was okay *not* to be okay). That was what I needed to hear. Instead, most of what I stumbled upon offered practical tips about sleep training or told me I should be treasuring every moment with you. There was always a bloody exclamation mark at the end of everything. *Your baby is now four months old! So much to look forward to this month! You might want to start thinking about weaning!* (I didn't want to think about weaning; I wanted a hot cup of tea and some sleep and to feel like myself again.)

There were blogs where motherhood looked *amazing* and glossy—just how I'd hoped it would be. Where everybody wore a Christmas jumper, nobody shat through their sleepsuit and everybody smiled all the time. They didn't help me.

I made a snap decision to start scribbling something of my own, and the blog was born. I frantically typed post after post about life at home with toddler Henry, about being pregnant with baby Jude, about baby groups, about trips out with you and all that came in between. It wasn't very glossy, and at times it was probably a bit ranty, but those nonglossy rantings were the reality for me at the time. I suppose the blog had become my modern-day diary.

It was never really *for* anyone, but people started to read it. Just a handful of people at first, and then a handful became hundreds, and hundreds became thousands, until millions of people had read my ramblings and I realized it was very much *out there*.

That realization came with a massive wobble, and I started to have doubts about baring my parenting soul. I really wanted to share my thoughts—the true ones. Yet as more people started to read those thoughts I began to have this niggling worry about what those thoughts would look like in black and white, forever etched on the World Wide Web. At some time or another, we all have thoughts we would rather forget. Sometimes those thoughts scare us; sometimes we are ashamed of them; sometimes they are embarrassing and we burn the diaries that housed them. Often these thoughts are personal to us and the last thing we want to do is immortalize them on the bloody Internet. What had I done?

But then I started taking stock of all the messages, all the comments, all the tweets and all the e-mails and I realized—holy shit!—the blog was *doing* something.

"Thank you," the messages said, "for making me feel normal."

"For making me laugh."

"For picking me up on a particularly bad week."

"For giving me the courage to admit this week's been crap and, no, I'm not enjoying every second."

Some of the messages from other mums (and a fair few dads) reduced me to tears. I have been given insights into their lives, into battles with postnatal depression, into their continual feelings of guilt and failure and their resigning themselves to the fact that they are very much alone. "I thought it must just be me," they told me.

I wanted to gather them all in one place and shout, *"It's not just you!"* through a megaphone, and that desire spurred me on to continue pouring out my honest assessment of day-to-day motherhood—an assessment which, remarkably, grew legs (and a front cover) and has allowed me to write my first-ever book.

I will no doubt look back at the blog and this book in years to come and think, "Jesus, you never stopped moaning, woman." I will no doubt look back and think, "But those years were over in a flash." I will no doubt look back and discover that I have written things I wish I hadn't written at all, things that were so very real at the time but which I would set a match to if I had the chance.

I may have called you slightly offensive things, like arseholes (sorry!), once or twice (I genuinely am sorry about that, though when you have little arseholes of your own, I'm sure you will understand); I may have reflected longingly on days spent working full-time; I may have wondered aloud why it wasn't all rainbows and cupcakes, why I was bored with park trips and baby groups and why I couldn't cherish every sodding second.

But I want you to know that there are so many moments I *have* cherished. Moments we have all cherished as a family. The cuddles we've had, the stories we've read, the people we've met, the places we've been, and the fact that the two of you and your dad have made me laugh every single day. I really wish I could offer you a favorably edited version of your earliest years, an edit where you would never have to find out that your mum swore quite a lot and sometimes cried. I wanted to be the glossy Christmas-jumper mum, I really did. I'm sorry if in any way I have let you down.

It's true that I haven't always felt like I am cut out for motherhood, but I have always known that nobody could love you more. You are beautiful and hilarious and totally bloody bonkers, and I am so very proud to be part of such a lovely family. I am proud to be your mum. Whatever else I achieve in life you two are my masterpieces and I will never have anything more important to my name.

Here's to us, my darlings.

I love you to the moon and back.

Mum xx

Introduction

THE UNMUMSY ONE

When I used to think about what my life with children would be like, I think I imagined my existing, child-free life with a couple of small people Photoshopped in: charming, small people with curls and cheeky, jam-smeared chops. It's not that I was startlingly ignorant—I knew there would be adjustments (less sleep, more nappies, less Jägerbomb drinking, more pram pushing). But, aside from maternity leave, the inevitable contact with another human's snot/sick/shit and the seemingly obligatory requirement to buy a VTech baby walker complete with plastic phone, I just didn't forecast my life changing that much at all.

I didn't forecast a hurricane.

But neither did Michael Fish in 1987, and look what happened there.

Needless to say, when Hurricane Baby hit in the winter of 2012, I was not prepared. Physically and materially speaking, I was pretty well equipped. Mentally and emotionally speaking, I was not. All the gear and no idea. That was me.

I have been asked several times what the hardest thing about that first baby hurricane was (and, indeed, what the hardest thing about having kids is now that I am the proud owner of two small humans, of whom only one is curly haired). I can describe at great length the sleep deprivation, the toddler tantrums in Debenhams and the frustration and boredom of watching *Escape to the Country* while feeding an insatiably hungry baby when all I really wanted was a shower.

Yes, those practical challenges were in themselves a test, but, over and above all of that, the biggest test by far has been the perpetual self-doubt.

Why am I not loving every second?
How come all the other mums are loving every second?
Is it possible that I'm somehow wired incorrectly, that I'm simply not up to the job?
This isn't what I thought it would be like at all.

When I typed "I want my old life back" into Google during a fraught three a.m. feed, I immediately deleted the search history on my phone. I was ashamed of myself because, mostly, I didn't want my old life back at all. I was head over heels in love with my bald bundle of baby-boy goodness and so very grateful that we had made a family. But there were occasions (like when I had already been up four times and the baby projectile-vomited in the Moses basket) when I couldn't stop myself from thinking, "What have we done?" Occasions when I couldn't stop myself from shouting, "I don't want to do this anymore. *It's fucking shit!*" at my husband, whose face told me the baby adventure wasn't panning out exactly as he had imagined either.

Several years later, in spite of the moments of magic still being interjected with moments that are just a bit shit, something incredible has happened. Despite flashes of continued self-doubt, I no longer truly believe I am alone in having these feelings. Why? Because it's impossible to ignore what has been an overwhelming response to my online account of those parenting highs and lows.

What started as a small handful of comments became hundreds; hundreds became thousands; and now, each and every day, my in-box is flooded with messages from parents whose experiences are not too dissimilar from my own. Parents who are beating themselves up for not loving every second—something they are sure they could do if only it wasn't all so bloody hard. I once scoffed when I heard parenting being described as "the hardest job in the world," but that was before I had lived it, before I had cut my own maternity leave short in favor of heading back to work part-time because, quite honestly, I couldn't hack being at home with the baby all day.

The name of my blog is often misconstrued. Being "mumsy" for me was never a negative concept. "Mumsy" sounded splendidly natural, happy and at ease with being a parent: all the things I wanted to be. So I called the blog "The *Un*mumsy Mum" because that was how I felt at the time: like a bit of a fraud, like

I didn't belong in the club. Writing down what was in my head and reading other parents commenting "Me, too" was truly remarkable and inspired me to keep going (both with the writing and with motherhood, as I've since had another child).

This book is for all those parents who have messaged me, and many more besides. It's for parents everywhere. Mums, dads, stepmums, stepdads, foster mums, foster dads, grannies, grandads and everyone in between who is in charge of bringing up a small person.*

I feel it necessary to point out that by no stretch of the imagination is this a parenting manual. If you were hoping for tips on getting your baby to nap in time for *Judge Rinder* or practical guidance about weaning, you might want to exchange my book for one of those "How to Grow a Child Who Isn't a Total Knobhead" titles.

This book won't tell you how to parent, what to buy, how you should feel. But I hope you find it useful nevertheless. More than anything, I hope it tells you that, whatever you are feeling, you can bet your bottom dollar that somebody else has been there and is feeling the same way, too.

So here it is. My uncensored account of going from zero to two children in the space of three years. The expectation versus the reality. The emotional highs and the "I just sieved a poo out of the bath with my hand" lows. The unapologetically honest account I wish I had come across when I was desperately scrolling through online baby forums at three a.m. I'm trying

---

*Dads and all the other males are more than welcome here, too, though I feel I should probably give you a heads-up that I do talk about blocked milk ducts and the state of things *down there*.

so hard not to use the word "journey" right now, because I hate it when people bang on about their sodding journeys. But, in the non-*X-Factor*-montage sense of the word, I suppose this *is* my journey.

On we go, then.

"When I look back to the vision I had of myself as a housewife *before* I actually had children (1950s-style, with my pinny on, my rosy-cheeked kids playing nicely while I had a civilized coffee with a friend who was sampling the freshly baked muffins I had made), I just laugh and wipe the snot smear off my leggings."

LARA, CHORLEY

Part One

WHAT HAVE WE DONE?

"Night feeds
are something special.
By 'special,' I mean they
are a bit shit."

Just the Two of Us

ALLOW ME TO set the prebaby scene. It's 2009.

I'm taking you back to 2009 because that year seems a fair representation of the prebaby us. It was the year we bought our first house and both had grown-up, serious jobs. James was occupying one of the many civil service jobs he's tried his hand at over the years, and I had just been promoted to relationship manager in an asset finance company, which, in practical terms, meant I spent lots of time driving around to farms in Devon financing machinery, and I bloody *loved* it.

We worked hard and played *sort of* hard. We occasionally rolled in drunk at two a.m. smelling of vodka and clutching shish kebabs, but, with the benefit of hindsight, we should have played harder. (I'm somehow mourning the raving I never did in Ibiza; not that I ever had any urge to get my trance on in an

Amnesia foam party, but I *could* have if I'd wanted to.) I didn't appreciate the extent of our freedom.

After an intense week of work, for us, the weekend revolved around a Pizza Hut delivery, bottles of wine and beer, the odd beach walk or excursion to a National Trust house (mainly for the cream tea) and copious amounts of sofa lounging, tea drinking and Jammie Dodger eating to the background hum of Sky Sports News. "Chores" were Hoovering out the car (which we could do in peace or while listening to the radio), grocery shopping (we bought what we fancied when we fancied it) and "cleaning the place," which took all of thirty minutes and consisted of sorting out piles of work clothes and tidying an already uncluttered living space.

Life was good, and we were happy. We were *settled*.

The following year, we tied the knot and started dabbling in that dangerous pastime I like to call Property Perusing. I'm sure it was all that talk of extra bedrooms and garages and friendly neighbors that prompted us to engage seriously for the first time in the Chat. There was only one chat to have by this stage, as we'd already gone down the pet route and rescued Floyd the Cat, who we treated very much like our baby.

The next level in our adult lives awaited.

I can't pinpoint or remember the exact "Shall we have a baby, then?" conversation, but I remember we agreed that I would come off the Pill and we would "see what happens." There is nothing casual about "seeing what happens." From the moment you are no longer *not* trying for a baby, you are very much trying for one.

I'm not sure what the rush was. There was certainly no biological rush, as I was just twenty-three at this point. We had all the time in the world to start procreating, but something instinctive told us it was the right time. We may have been just a few months into married life but, by this stage, we were a full seven years into our relationship. I was just *sixteen* when we first got together (at a nightclub on an industrial estate: the romance of fairy tales—I know).

All of a sudden, I became hyperaware of babies in buggies and pregnancy bumps on the bus. Despite my continued enjoyment of work, wine and uninterrupted Friday-night takeaways, more than anything else I wanted to be a mum.

I guessed it would happen straightaway.

It didn't happen straightaway.

In fact, ten months into the whole "I think I'm ovulating. Can you pause *Top Gear* and come upstairs, please?" debacle, we'd become slightly disheartened with the bi-daily shagathons and leg holding in the air (me, not James, who never once lay with his legs in the air for ten minutes to discourage gravity).

Then, suddenly, we had other things to concentrate on because we'd just completed the sale of our house and secured a new one with that extra bedroom and garage. Hurrah! It was a chaotic time, as we had only a couple of weeks off work to pack up, move house *and* prepare for a week's holiday in Kos— a holiday I'd booked prior to knowing we'd be moving that month. So, in a state of mostly unpacked but not quite organized household disorder, we found ourselves getting ready to leave for a road trip to Cardiff airport. I ran myself a bath (to take care of the essential holiday hair removal), and while I fannied around in the bedroom waiting for the tub to fill up, I just had this *feeling* that I was coming on my period: achy legs, slight tummy churn. You probably don't need to know the workings of my menstrual cycle (you'll undoubtedly know far too much about me as it is when you've finished reading this book), but I never really had regular periods, something we had been told might make it difficult for us to conceive, something which would have made it all the more sensible to pack tampons as a precaution for a week in a bikini.

I don't know whether the feeling was in some way different from the usual premenstrual rigmarole or whether I just wanted clearance to drink my body weight in dodgy Greek ouzo, but something prompted me to grab a pregnancy test out of my knicker drawer and wee on it. I shouted down to James, "I think I'm coming on my period, but I've done a test just in case, so I have the all clear to drink wine."

James came back upstairs. I was totally naked by this point (about to get in the bath, as I say), hovering over said stick of fortune. "Well, what does it say?" he asked.

"There are two lines. It's a plus. It says I'm pregnant. Fuck."

"Fuck," he echoed. "Are you sure? Do another one!"

"I can't! I don't need another wee."

I then sat in the bath, trying to digest the possible parenthood news, while James went to get me a pint of water so I could flush out some more urine. I did two further tests.

One test could be a fluke.

Two tests: still questionable.

Three tests: well, three tests showed irrefutably that I was *with child*.

Holy mother of chuffing God, there was a baby in there.

And we were about to whisk him or her off to Kos for a stay in what turned out to be the shittiest hotel we'd been to in all our years, with a shit "beach" and shit food. Add to that an overall sense of shittiness brought about by knowing that not only had we rejected a villa in Tuscany but we were now also *not* enjoying our last holiday as a twosome.

The saving grace of that holiday-which-was-a-bit-shit (have I told you how shit it was? I feel the need to reiterate this point, as it was James who said no to Tuscany, for cost-saving reasons) was that we were carrying around our baby secret. We were going to be parents, and we beamed from ear to ear.

According to the BabyCenter pregnancy app we had downloaded on the way to the airport, I was already seven weeks pregnant. The absence of my period had not alerted us because that, in itself, was not unusual. I'd had no other symptoms and had therefore been drinking Pinot Grigio and not taking folic acid for the first seven weeks of our fetus's existence, something I planned to rectify as soon as we got back to Blighty and I could ram-raid Boots for mum-to-be supplies.

So there we were, in our ghetto sunshine hotel, discussing baby names and nurseries and telling ourselves we really shouldn't get carried away until we'd confirmed everything was all right while at the same time getting completely carried away about our little potato. Finding out I was pregnant for the first time was pretty amazing. It was scary and daunting, too, but mostly it was amazing.

I'll forever hold an image in my mind of our tanned and

excited faces in the car on the way back from Cardiff airport, scoffing M&S sandwiches and Percy Pigs (and Pals) from the service station. Smug about our little secret. We knew we were on the cusp of something pretty life changing.

The reality, of course, as we gaily chomped on Percy and his Pals, was that we knew nothing at all.

Am I Glowing Yet?

As you know, I am writing as the proud (though slightly overwhelmed) owner of two children. I have therefore spent eighteen months of my life incubating small people. (Total for both pregnancies, I mean; I don't have anything approaching the 640-day gestation of an African elephant because if I did, I would, quite frankly, never have coped. Can you imagine the pelvic pressure and gin withdrawal after 640 days?) Still, eighteen months equates to approximately 5 percent of my life (to date) spent "with child," and, when people ask me how I found my pregnancy adventure, I generally offer the same, uncomplicated response: "It was a bit crap."

I really *tried* to enjoy it. Mostly, I think, I felt compelled to treasure the experience because I was so mindful of pregnancy being a blessing, mindful that there are so many other couples who can't conceive, or have lost a baby. I have always known that getting pregnant and carrying two healthy babies to full term makes us a remarkably lucky family.

And there were bits I *did* enjoy. Like all the buzzy excitement surrounding the new addition, the magic of feeling the first kicks, and hearing the heartbeat at the midwife appointments. Discussing names (slightly less fun after we'd made the mistake of sharing name ideas with friends and family, who were surprisingly forthright about our short list); dragging James to antenatal classes (where we tried and failed to act like grown-ups during the demonstration of the doll moving down the birth canal); shopping for baby clothes; painting the nursery and framing my favorite quote from *The Twits* to add a bit of Roald Dahl wisdom to the walls.

I marveled at my body's ability to grow a small person, twice.

But treasure *every* moment I could not.

I quickly tired of sticking my head down the loo to throw up after my evening meal. I became fed up with practically pissing myself every time I climbed the stairs or rolled over in bed because my bladder had been restricted to the size of a Borrower's. I spent the last six weeks of pregnancy number two sleeping (or, rather, not sleeping) propped up on the sofa, unable to get comfy, watching reruns of *The X-Files*. And, on top of the pregnancy incontinence and slightly sicky burps, I was fed up with hearing the same old shite, those same old myths and superstitions:

"All that sickness suggests this one is definitely a girl!" Clearly.

"The first baby is never on time!" He was on time.

"As your first was on time, your second will be early!" He was seven days late.

"I can tell just by looking at the bump you're having a big baby!" Henry was six pounds, thirteen ounces.

Above all, I was a bit pissed off and disillusioned about the pregnancy legend of the Glow.

I wasn't glowing.

But it would come, right? Because I, for one, had bought into the legend and was excited about my impending glow. I just had to get through the sicky and awkward podgy-but-not-quite-preggers stage of the first trimester (the "shitemester") and I'd be on the home straight to the promised land of shiny hair, radiant skin and a neat and tidy bump displayed proudly under attractive maternity dresses. It became a long-standing joke: "Am I glowing yet?"

I never fucking glowed.

Instead, I found I was vomity, sweaty and permanently tired. My skin was gray and slightly zitty—less English rose glow and more hungover pubescent-teenager shine. The "bump" I had looked forward to sporting under a Topshop tea dress developed into more of a tire of pregnant chub around my middle, spreading slowly to unsuspecting areas like my arms. And chins. In many ways, I quite liked my preggers body—I put on more than three stone with each pregnancy, and there is something quite liberating about thinking, "Sod it, what difference is another slice of carrot cake going to make?"

But glowing I was not. Though I should note that I have met some quite glowy mums-to-be in Topshop tea dresses, so

I can't deny that it happens. It just didn't happen in the 5 percent of my lifetime I have spent pregnant. (I'm not at *all* bitter.)

There were, however, two things I'd heard about pregnancy—two quirks, if you will (things I had generally dismissed as "a load of old tosh")—that I can in fact verify as true, having experienced them firsthand.

The first was nesting.

"Nesting," as a term, is quite misleading, I think, because it conjures up images of decluttering, decorating and making sure things are just so. The nesting I found myself absorbed in was much less about decluttering and more about disinfecting. Of ridding the house of all dust, grime and odors and leaving behind the soft scents of Cif Cream (Original) and Windowlene.

I could not get enough of cleaning products. They just smelled so good. The Cillit Bang advert where "Barry Scott" obliterates shower scum before declaring, "Bang! And the dirt is gone!" was practically a turn-on at one point.

At the height of my cleaning obsession (which was far worse with Jude), I was spraying and scrubbing my kitchen worktops at least three times a day—and that was the most ordinary of my cleaning activities. Skirting-board bleaching, cupboard disinfecting, pulling the fridge out to clean behind it, door washing, wall cleaning—I once washed the *external* walls and downstairs outside windows with Flash power spray before instructing my father-in-law to do the same to the upstairs windows while he was up a ladder clearing the guttering. I also asked James to pull the TV stand out twice in the same week because I hadn't managed to blitz all the dust the first time and I couldn't relax until I had blitzed *all of the bloody dust.*

Nobody argued with me when I was eight months pregnant, because they had clocked my crazed look and feared I would climb a ladder/attempt to move a forty-two-inch TV on my own. They were right to be slightly fearful. There were spells of comedy, but I had become a nightmare to live with. One time, I paused our Friday-night film to strip the cushion covers and put them straight in the wash. Because you just can't bring new life into a house with unwashed cushion covers. Another time, James put some leftover lasagna—which was ever so slightly leaking out of its dish—into my newly disinfected fridge. "Lasagnagate," we named that particular meltdown, because I cried for half an hour before getting the surface cleaner back out. Poor James.

Obviously, I can see *now* that shedding tears over lasagna residue was highly irrational—I was being ridiculous. But it felt very rational at the time. In fact, it was one of the most instinctive and compulsive feelings I've ever had—I *needed* to clean the nest.

It wasn't until a couple of weeks after the birth that I could walk down the cleaning aisle in Tesco without attempting to sniff-test how citrus fresh the products were. (Barry doesn't do it for me sexually anymore, just so we're clear.)

The second pregnancy-related quirk I was hit with was cravings. Less so in my first pregnancy—unless you count McChicken Sandwich Meals, and I've been craving those for the best part of twenty-nine years. But certainly in the latter part of my second pregnancy I developed quite a hard-core craving for ice. Not icy drinks or ice lollies but *ice cubes*. Popped straight from the freezer tray into my mouth and crunched one by one as if they were peanut M&M's. For every tray I demolished I would freeze another so I would never run out. Because running out would have been catastrophic to my emotional well-being. Apparently, ice-cube crunching can be symptomatic of iron deficiency and is very common in pregnancy. Whatever it was that compelled me to crunch up to fifty ice cubes a day, it was bloody odd. Just the thought of it makes my teeth hurt.

So my pregnancy adventure was nothing if not interesting. (And a blessing.)

(And just a little bit crap.)

"When I was pregnant, I visited Toys 'R' Us for the first time. This is the conversation I heard from a family coming out as I went in:

"'I want a Minion!'

"'You're not having a Minion.'

"'But I *want* a Minion! Waaaahhh!'

"'You didn't even know what a bloody Minion was before you went in there!'

"I will never forget this."

MARIE, EXETER

I Am Pushing!

CHILDBIRTH FASCINATES ME. Despite having been slightly traumatized sixteen years ago when I witnessed Sarah-Lou give birth on *Coronation Street*, I had more recently become a big fan of *One Born Every Minute*, and I was looking forward to having my own birth story to tell. I was also looking forward to bidding farewell to the surface spraying, vomiting and ice crunching.

Labor is a proper rite of passage into motherhood, isn't it? Whichever way the baby comes out (via the sunroof or down the lady garden slide), it's the point at which you gain entry to the Club. I couldn't wait to earn my "I've Given Birth" badge, and I planned to wear it proudly to baby groups, where I would exchange knowing nods with other mums who had birthed tiny (and on occasion not-so-tiny) humans from their bodies.

I now have *two* stories to share, and when people ask me, "How was the birth?" or "Was it really awful?" I give my honest assessment, which is this: it entirely depends on which birth you're asking me about, because I'm fairly certain the same woman did not give birth to my two children.

If I had written this chapter directly after the birth of Henry, it would have been a pretty positive one. If I had written this chapter directly after the birth of Jude, it would have been a very short one (probably just "Holy shit!"). This leaves me with an interesting quandary. What should I share with you in this chapter? How should I pitch it when I am not even sure I have made sense of my feelings yet?

So I have settled on simply sharing the two births as I remember them and reflecting honestly on a few of the thoughts I've had since. Here we go, then.

The Birth of Henry

After a false start bang on his due date (February 13), I went into labor properly on Valentine's Day. It all started pretty calmly, with James monitoring the regularity of my contractions using the contraction-timer app on his iPhone as I sat bouncing on the exercise ball in front of *Lorraine*. (I bloody love Lorraine; she's been there through many an important life moment, and it seems only right that she was party to the onset of my first labor.) We engaged in endless chats about whether we'd packed everything in the hospital bag (me and James, I mean, not me and Lorraine). I'd unpacked and repacked the bag at least ten times because something I'd read on the Internet said I needed two packs of maternity pads, and that couldn't be right, surely? Then I had "the show," which, despite sounding quite fun (and making me want to do jazz hands), was, in reality, gross. Just to be sure it was indeed showtime, I ended up *showing* it to James, who was, understandably, disgusted. During that same hour (I think *Jeremy Kyle* was on by this point), my waters broke. It was all pretty textbook.

It didn't stay textbook for long, though, and I started vomiting quite badly. Cue James directing said vomit away from the new sofas and, in return, me giving him the death stare for worrying about the sofa fabric when I was preparing to expel three kilograms of baby out of my fandango. To add to the excitement, I could tell by looking at the color of what was coming out of my fandango that something wasn't right.

"I think the baby's shat in my waters—they mentioned something about this at those classes!"

I therefore wasn't at all surprised when, after waddling into the midwife-led birthing unit (the one we'd carefully selected for the least clinical and most naturally empowering birth experience that wasn't our home), we were packed straight off to the hospital.

Alongside the baby's in utero dirty protest, my blood pressure was rocketing, and by the time I had my first examination at the Royal Devon & Exeter, the situation was confirmed: I had preeclampsia.

Shit.

Preeclampsia is some serious business, which explains why there was a multitude of important people in the room whose brows were furrowed at all times. Apart from the contractions, which had intensified beyond the point of my being able to chat comfortably with James about the choice of snacks he'd packed in *his* hospital bag (ha!), I was actually *feeling* all right. I was finding it more tolerable than I'd expected and, following a gloriously pain-free couple of hours (thanks to an epidural) and after my mistaken intuition that I was about to poo myself, baby Henry arrived naturally without too much fuss. If I had been filmed for an episode of *OBEM*, I would have been quite proud.

"You did so well, babe!" James told me. I really did. I kept my shit together (both figuratively and literally) and subsequently told curious friends, "It really wasn't that bad!"

The Birth of Jude

Two years and seven months later I went into labor for the second time and became a total monster. If I had been awarded a medal for composure in childbirth the first time, it would have been stripped from me the second time. I became *that* woman on *OBEM*. The one you sit watching with your cup of tea and five Custard Creams, thinking, "For God's sake, woman, pull yourself together!"

I lost the plot.

It's difficult to pinpoint the moment it all went a bit tits up because, on paper, unlike during the first birth, *I* was all right. There was no blood-pressure crisis or risk of having a seizure, and everyone at the hospital seemed quite chilled out. Everyone, that is, except me.

I had failed to prepare for the possibility of a trickier birth, instead wholeheartedly buying into the whole second-birth-is-easier promise. There was no doubt in my mind that I would boss it, which, in hindsight, was a foolish error. The reality was that the birth of young Jude took almost twice as long and was considerably more painful. The calm and collected woman from birth one failed to show up for birth two. She sent her twin sister instead, who was a bit of a moron.

James's assessment of Jude's delivery (which kind of erased the reigning "You did so well, babe!" praise) was: "You were mental. I've never seen anything like it."

Throughout the labor I switched from hysterical to withdrawn. I sploshed into the birthing pool with the expectation of laboring serenely while submerged in water, but it was less than an hour before I ungracefully heaved myself out, demanding *"something that works!"* When James dared to suggest I should stick the pool out for a bit longer, I snapped angrily at him that I needed "more than a giant fucking bath."

I puffed on gas and air for a bit, felt slightly dizzy and lightheaded, and then discarded the mouthpiece in a sulk. I wanted an epidural. I was talked out of an epidural. The wonderful (and bloody patient) midwife (Trish, I think her name was; we'll call her Trish) explained that the baby could arrive in just an hour or two. The epidural might slow things down. It might lead to an unnecessary stay in hospital the following day. James agreed—I had probably just reached the Wall, and our boy would be with us in no time.

Diamorphine arrived. I had two doses of that bad boy before becoming sleepy and unresponsive. I had been awake for twenty-four hours by this point and was so bloody exhausted that I fell asleep (sitting up) between contractions, moaning like a wounded animal. At one stage, James informs me, I refused to communicate for several hours and sat silently rocking on the bed, occasionally glaring at him and poor Trish. I mean, WTF? (In my defense, I genuinely wondered whether I was dying from the pain. I can recall thinking that it would be a relief to die. Irrational doesn't even come close.) My contractions were wearing off due to low blood-sugar levels—I needed a sugary drink. I refused the sugary drink.

And then the pièce de résistance of my birthing performance came when I was ten centimeters dilated and I went on the most pointless strike of my life and refused to push.

"I want an epidural!" I wailed at nobody in particular, and was quite rightly ignored, because that ship had sailed about five centimeters earlier.

"I want a cesarean!"

"I want to die!"

Yep.

Everyone became concerned. Trish had a stern word.

According to James, I then pretended to push, mumbling, "I *am* pushing!" while blatantly failing to direct any effort downward. I must have picked up my game, though, and pushed for real eventually, because, after three hours—and after feeling the familiar sensation of trying to shit a cannonball—baby Jude finally arrived.

What a relief.

I remember cradling him in his little towel, thinking he looked proper lovely and pink, just like he should (and not at all bothered by his mother's reluctance to help him out of the birth canal). I was so elated it was all over.

And then the placenta got stuck.

FFS. I had no idea that was even a possibility. The placenta never gets stuck when people give birth on telly, does it? Where the hell *is* the placenta on TV births? I've never seen a woman give birth on *Holby* and then witnessed the medical team jabbing her in the leg with an injection to bring on the afterbirth, before carting off what looks like a giant stingray (if a stingray had the texture of internal organs). I sure as hell haven't ever seen a placenta get stuck. But, sure enough, mine did. There was talk of spinals and the operating theater, and several attempts to manipulate it were made before one doctor succeeded where all others had failed. I am not going to describe exactly how this happened, but the adjective James used later to describe what he witnessed in that moment was "brutal," so you probably get the picture.

And then it really was over. We enjoyed a delightful round of tea and toast and stared some more at our beautiful bundle wrapped up snugly in his plastic crib. He was still unnamed at this point (I wanted to call him Wilf). Following a very wobbly hot shower and plenty of "Christ, that was awful, wasn't it?" conversations, we left the hospital, and our life as a newly extended family of four began.

I HAVE SUBSEQUENTLY laughed about the chaos of Jude's delivery ("I was a nightmare!"; "Trust me to have a stubborn placenta! LOL!"), but the truth is it knocked me for six and, until now, I have avoided thinking about it. In many ways it undid all the positives I'd taken from Henry's birth, which is a shame. I don't watch *OBEM* anymore but, if I did, I am certain I would no longer feel like slapping some sense into the mums having a meltdown, because I get it now. They are not being irrational, they just don't know what to do.

Having given quite a lot of thought to what I would do differently if I ever had another one (stand down, James, this is as hypothetical as what I'd do if we won the lottery), I have come up with the following two courses of action:

First, I would research hypnobirthing. I have seen and read some amazing things about hypnobirthing and, at the heart of it, there seems to be an emphasis on feeling empowered and maintaining *control* (something I definitely lost during birth two). There has to be a reason why celeb and nonceleb mums alike are raving about it and, if I had my pregnancy time again, I'd give it a shot. Nothing ventured, nothing gained, right?

Second, if ever I found myself in that same amount of pain again, I would press more firmly for an epidural. Every centimeter of my body was crying out for help at that point, and I really regretted not having one. Yes, I know there are advantages to going natural and drug free, but it turns out I much preferred the birth with all of the drugs. I'm not ashamed of that—there are no prizes for managing without and, if I had my pregnancy time again, I would hook myself up to an epidural the moment I discovered two blue lines on the pregnancy test. I'm joking (kind of).

I have heard and read so many birth stories over the last few years, ranging from traumatic and scary emergency C-sections to unbelievably rapid deliveries in hospital car parks, and the more I read, the more I am certain that no two labors are the same. Every birth is unique, every woman is an individual, and some women (me included) behave differently to *themselves* in differing situations.

Part of my reluctance to look back at Jude's delivery stems from embarrassment, I think. It's one thing rocking on all fours with all your bits out, but it's quite another shouting panicked expletives as you rock on all fours with all your bits out. All things considered, though, I have no doubt that the midwives have seen it all before, so perhaps there is no need to beat ourselves up if we have a bit of a meltdown.

Though, Trish, if you're reading this, I would like to say that I'm sorry for scowling, shouting and smacking your hand away when you tried to check the baby's heartbeat with that Doppler thingy. Basically, I'm sorry for being a bit of a twat. I would also like to say thank you for seeing past my twattishness and safely delivering a beautiful little boy to take home to my beautiful not-so-little boy. You do an unbelievably special job. Respect of the highest order, midwife folk!

He Can't Be F***ing Hungry!

I DON'T THINK ANYTHING prepares you for the trauma of night feeds. Well, I don't think anything prepares you for the constant day feeds either (within hours of leaving the hospital, I had ascertained that my new life would be dictated by milk), but, my God, night feeds are something special. By "special," I mean they are a bit shit. My mental preparation (first time around) was to tell myself that I would be knackered but that I would catch up on lost sleep during the day. I quite simply had *no idea*. It's never just about the lost sleep; it's about having to undertake frustrating tasks several times a night without having *had* any sleep. Feeding, nappy changing, winding, vomit cleaning, sheet stripping, more nappy changing . . . I can recall, during one of many feeds, staring at the ceiling in a trance, wondering if it was possible to die from tiredness and concluding that if it was, my time had come. It seemed to me that sleep must have been regulating hidden unstable tendencies lurking in my subconscious for the preceding twenty-five years, and that lack of sleep had introduced the Hyde to my Jekyll. How I longed for sleep! Never before had I understood the expression "I'd give my right arm for—," but in the thick of sleep deprivation I would have given my right leg as well.

In an attempt to further maximize our chances of a solid four hours' sleep (when did four hours become a good amount of sleep? *When did it?*), James and I trialed white noise as a soother. First we downloaded a whole album of white noise from iTunes. Rock and roll. Later, when times got desperate and we allowed ourselves to be taken in by miracle baby products on Amazon, we purchased a bear stuffed with a white-noise player. I think it was of some benefit—we used to sleep with it between us and whack it when the threat of baby wakeage was imminent. Who knows, to be honest, but falling asleep to a medley of fan noises and gentle waves certainly became the norm in our house. So much so, we willingly engaged in middle-of-the-night post-nappy-changing conversations about our favorite tracks: "Move it to the next one. I like the gentle rain best, don't you?" We had lost the plot by this point.

You pray it will get better and, usually, eventually, it does. Until such a time, you endure the night feeds in a series of desperately shit stages.

The Night Feed in Five Psychological Stages

1. Hope

As the baby drifts off to sleep, sandwiched between the soft bunny comforter and the white-noise contraption, you allow yourself to dream that *this could be the night*. Tonight will be different.

2. Denial

You have been asleep for no more than five minutes, and he is awake. This cannot *be*, you think. You ignore the frantic crying and whack the white-noise thingy in a last-ditch attempt to settle him. This is a fruitless exercise, but you have not yet come to terms with the fact that he wants feeding. *Again.* "Just go back to sleep," you say quietly (to nobody in particular, while sobbing).

3. The Standoff

Now that you have established that he is well and truly awake (he is the color of a beetroot; half the street can hear his screams), you lie perfectly still. Your stillness sends a body-language message to your husband: I am asleep; I am not getting up. You pray he will get up. He doesn't even stir. Marvelous. Sometimes, you commence the standoff only halfheartedly, because you need to get up for a wee, so the game is already over.

4. Rage

You angrily turn the night-light on, "accidentally" kick said husband in the ribs and declare, "How is he fucking hungry? Why is he being such a dick? This is ridiculous! Fucking *ridiculous!*" as you whisk the baby out of his cot and commence the feed (sighing loudly). If your husband does wake during this stage, he can expect to hear you declare, "Never having another one," or, alternatively, "Having another one was a mistake," and/or *"I fucking hate my life!"* If he doesn't wake up, you will be so annoyed with his snoring (breathing) you will want to punch him in the face.

5. Guilt

The baby smiles at you. Between the swearing and the start of divorce proceedings, that little bundle of agitated loudness starts cooing and gurgling. You now feel awful for having blamed him for ruining your life. And calling him a dick. So, while feeding, you whisper, "Shhhh. It's all right. Is that nice? Do you like your milkies?" etc., while reflecting on what a terrible mother you are and searching Netmums for threads where other people admit to calling their babies dicks. (You will never find such threads, which further reinforces your conclusion that you are, in fact, a terrible accident of motherhood.)

Eventually, after a through-the-suit poo explosion, you all settle back to sleep, where you have approximately fifty-five minutes before this hope-denial-standoff-rage-guilt cycle of doom starts again . . .

I should point out that James did more than his fair share of night feeds, but we came to an agreement early on that I would do the lion's share of night duty while I was "off" on maternity leave—after all, he would be driving to work in the morning. I wasn't at all jealous that he would get to go to work in the morning. Not at all . . .

I think people reflect very differently on their experiences of doing the night feeds. I have been offered some reasonable advice along the way, like "It gets easier" (it really does), "It's not forever" (it really isn't) and "Just take it one night at a time" (that's all you can do, ultimately). But I have also read some absolute bollocks about making sure you *treasure* the night feeds, *cherish* them, and I want to make it clear that you are under no obligation to find enjoyment here. I mean, it's more than possible that, between the sleep deprivation and the hysteria, you just might encounter some magical moments, moments of calm when the rest of the world is sleeping and just the two of you are awake. You might discover it's your special time for bonding. But it's also fine if you make no such discovery—for me, said special times for bonding were simply more welcome during the daytime. I never resented my boys for waking me in the night—I mean, I did at the time, in that moment when I called them dicks (my bad), but in the grander scheme of things I didn't. Babies need a lot of food, and I never truly expected them to sleep for twelve hours. I knew I would have to endure those night feeds—all things considered, that turned out to be one of the least surprising parts about having a baby. But it didn't mean they were any less hard. "You'll never get this time again," people warned me after hearing me complain about night-feed tiredness. Well, thank fuck for that, quite frankly. I don't want that time again.

If you are reading this as a brand-new parent or parent-to-be, I'm not going to bullshit you with any guarantees. Having a baby is much like buying a secondhand car—you are willingly entering into a lottery you have no control over, and all you can do is hope for the best. I know somebody whose "baby" did not sleep through the night until he was, in fact, almost three, and somebody else whose baby slept through after just a few weeks. We were unlucky in the sleep stakes the first time (Henry woke up *hourly* for an awfully long time, and it nearly broke me), but we struck gold with Jude, who simply loves sleeping, despite having been treated to the exact same routine as his brother. Just make sure you exercise caution when you inevitably enter into the Baby Olympics at playgroup (whose baby sleeps the longest, whose baby has the strongest neck, whose baby clapped first, *yawn*), because the concept of "sleeping through" is not uniform. I once met a mum who declared that her baby was sleeping through at five weeks. I wanted to smack her in the face (the mum, not the baby, just to be clear). Turns out her concept of "sleeping through" was midnight until five a.m. ("Midnight is when we go to bed; five a.m. is just an early-morning start.") Perhaps there's something to be said for that level of positivity, but I beg to differ that her baby was *sleeping through*, though I certainly wanted to punch her slightly less after that. Give or take an hour, seven p.m. to seven a.m. has always been our definition of sleeping through.

Aim high, my friends.

"Becoming a mum for the first time was the biggest
shock I think I've ever had. As a teacher I thought, I've got this,
how hard can a baby be in comparison to thirty fourteen-year-olds
who do not want to learn? How bloody wrong was I? Between sleep deprivation,
trying and failing to breastfeed and recovering from a C-section, I couldn't
believe what I'd done to myself and my life in having a baby. I felt
shitty for hating being a mum to a newborn, and then I felt
guilty and hated myself—it was just a huge
roundabout of emotions."
ANONYMOUS

The Good, the Bad and the Lumpy: Breastfeeding Highs and Lows

I HAVE DISCOVERED THAT most mums have a breastfeeding story to tell. Their personal breastfeeding *journey*, as it were (there's that word again; bloody hell). When I was pregnant, I found most of the breastfeeding literature to be quite dull—factual "feeding your baby" blurb accompanied by images from the 1980s depicting the correct positioning of the baby's mouth around the areola and warnings about mastitis. This was all highly practical and really rather necessary when I later found myself staring at a brand-new baby who was gumming any skin he could find, including his dad's hairy chest. I was relieved to be well versed in the health benefits, the cost benefits and all the stuff they put in the leaflets. But I was also eager to hear some more candid tales, the less leaflet-friendly stuff. What was breastfeeding really *like*?

So here's what I have learned about breastfeeding. You know, on my *journey*.

At First, It Is Bloody Hard Work

I found breastfeeding in the early days pretty relentless. The first few weeks are a shock to the system anyway, and having a small human welded to your nipples for an apparent *eternity* is exhausting. "Feeding on demand" does what it says on the tin and, during the first couple of months with both boys, I felt like a slave to lactation. With Henry, there were times when he fed for an hour and less than an hour later wanted feeding again . . . for another hour. I remember reaching the point of no return, the deliriously tired point where you laugh and cry at the same time, sobbing to James that the baby was on a bender ("He's binge drinking!"). On those days it was pretty painful, and I faffed around with nipple shields, creams and alternative positioning, reclining ungracefully on the sofa in an attempt to "bring baby to breast" in all manner of interesting ways (remembering what I'd read in those leaflets I'd been given).

I saw a breastfeeding counselor, who advised that I could try viewing each feed as the baby's opportunity to have a three-course meal. Breast one could be his starter and main (to allow for two "letdowns") and, if he finished those, I could offer the second breast "as dessert." This was actually really helpful advice, but I just wanted to scream at everyone. I wanted to mourn the loss of my existence outside of sitting on the sofa with my breasts out. I wanted to shout about how unfair it was that *I* never finished a meal unless James cut everything into fork-sized chunks, and when I finally did get a break for the jackpot of forty winks, it was invariably cut short by the phrase of doom: "I think he's hungry again." *Arghhhhhh!*

It's Also Bloody Handy

At many other times, the boobs were in favor. All hail the boobs! Because in my tired, disheveled and, frankly, zombified state, those boobs were one less thing to worry about packing in the changing bag. Wherever we were, there was milk. Not too hot, not too cold, but just right. Hoo-bloody-ray. My boobs were like my weapon of choice, something always in my locker. One time, when baby Jude threatened to have a meltdown on a train, I unclipped my bra, literally shoved a boob in his face and continued to read *Heat* magazine while relaxing against the window. It is one of those vivid moments when I recall thinking, "Thank God for that." Another "breastfeeding is the bomb" realization came when, after switching to bottles, we found ourselves dangerously low on formula reserves one Sunday afternoon when all the shops had shut ("You said *you* were getting some!") and, furthermore, when we totted up the £40+ it was costing us each month to buy our tubs of Cow & Gate. Breastfeeding is free, and if that doesn't make it a little bit incredible I don't know what does.

It's an Interesting Experience . . .

You get told all about hand expressing and breast pumps and the like at antenatal classes, but the everyday reality of these things turned out to be more hysterical than I could ever have imagined. I had a proper good bash at expressing the first time around because I wanted James to join in with some of the feeds. It wasn't that I didn't enjoy breastfeeding . . . though I didn't *much* enjoy it. (I never cherished the feeds in the way I know some mums do, but I have long since made peace with my lack of moment cherishing.) It was just that the prospect of breast milk in a bottle seemed like a win-win situation, and I couldn't wait to crack out the pump and share the ~~burden~~ joy. Amazing things, those electric pumps, but, Jesus Christ, it was all a bit ridiculous. I would sit on the sofa with one nipple attached to a suction cone (being milked) and the other nipple resting in a plastic shell (to catch the extra milk that was leaking from the neglected boob, which had not registered that it was the other boob's turn). Having spent the previous three years financing agricultural machinery—parlors and robotic milkers aplenty—I developed a newfound respect for dairy cows through my personal experience of being milked while watching *This Morning*. James often joked about the regularity of boob exposure in the living room ("There they are again!"), and he was right. It became so commonplace to have them out that some days I didn't bother putting them back in.

And then there was the Incident. A particular breastmilk-expressing episode that neither of us has quite recovered from.

I woke up one morning with breasts that were more than a little bit engorged—they were like lumpy boulders. I started to feel all hot and bothered, fearing that mastitis was approaching. Usually, when lumps and bumps developed I could "sort myself out" by kneading my boobs gently with my fingers to clear what I assumed were blocked milk ducts. Sometimes, the relief of the next feed would be overwhelming and my boobs would be ready to explode by the time the poor boys copped a mouthful. On this particular day in 2012 I knew I had gone past the point of self-rescue and, after trying and failing to "massage out the lumps," I called James up to the bedroom for what has definitely gone down as the most interesting moment of our marriage to date.

He found me sitting on the bed in just my pants, surrounded by towels and warm flannels, with boobs to rival Katie Price's in her Jordan heyday (albeit lumpy and slightly inflamed).

"You're going to have to hand-express me."

[Face of disbelief.] "You're shitting me."

"No, I actually need you to hand-express me. I can't get the right angle to massage both boobs in full, and the pump won't attach now they're so massive. It's really hurting."

"Fucking hell. Right."

And so it came to pass that my husband sat behind me on the bed and milked me. In a completely nonsexual way (because there is nothing sexy about lactation*), it gave me the

---

*I should note that data captured from my blog regarding search keywords (i.e., what people have searched for before being referred to my blog) did, worryingly, point toward an underground subsection of the great British public who do find lactation sexy. I'm pretty sure the person who searched "lactation fuck breast milk shower" would have been disappointed by my blog post.

greatest sense of relief I've ever felt. We drenched at least two towels in breast milk before admiring my back-to-normal boob structure, high-fiving and heading back downstairs for a cup of tea. That's marriage right there, for better or for worse.

Bitty Fashion Is Not Always the Tits

Many breastfeeding mums do a sterling job of looking glam all the time and manage to dress like they haven't given up on life. I do think that finding trendy, boob-accessible stuff on the high street is getting easier (dungarees are now in fashion, for starters), but I'm not overly imaginative when it comes to fashion, and there were times when I just wanted to choose an outfit without easy boob access in mind, when I fancied wearing something other than loose tops, wrap dresses, button-down tunics or jumpers with "secret" feeding panels (there is no secret: I can spot a JoJo nursing top a mile off), or when I was fed up with leaking breasts and the risk of waking up in a wet T-shirt because a breast pad had got sodden or dislodged between night feeds. I had almost forgotten those moments of midnight breast leakage and wardrobe agonizing until my friend texted me midfeed to tell me she was fed up with squeezing her oversize boobs into "bitty fashion"(!) and "smelling like an old fridge." She's a keeper.

Sometimes, It Doesn't Work Out

There's an awful lot of pressure on mums to breastfeed. In light of all the benefits, I understand why encouraging mums to do so is really important. Sometimes, an expert pair of eyes is helpful in assessing the baby's position or to offer advice around greedy-baby syndrome (I think the technical term is "cluster feeding" and the explanation is *always* a growth spurt). Sometimes, just a boost is welcome, somebody to say, "Keep going, it gets easier!"

But I have also read messages from mums so desperate to carry on breastfeeding that they have cried through the sheer pain of feeds, continuing with bleeding nipples and an inadequate milk supply because the thought of "giving up" is somehow worse. As if they have been told, "Keep going, it gets easier!" one too many times and have started to wonder what *not* keeping going would mean. What it would say about them and their maternal capabilities.

I vowed to give you my honest experience of parenting, and I don't think breastfeeding should be an exception, though, for some reason, I feel like there is an elephant in the room as I write this, shaking his trunk at my blasphemous suggestion that breast isn't always best . . .

I honestly *would* recommend breastfeeding. I have lived it, and I am a fan. But if you are reading this and the bad stuff has struck a chord in any way, I just want to put it out there that it is absolutely *not* the end of the world if it doesn't work out, if you need/want/have to formula feed instead, because how your baby is fed does not determine your parent-awesomeness rating. Sometimes, mums deserve the best option, too. I'm pretty sure even the elephant would agree with that one.

"I have loved, carried and nurtured
this baby inside me for nine months, I have spent every moment
of my life thinking about him since I knew he was on his way—take your
vitamins, don't drink, don't smoke, eat right, exercise, do what's best
for baby, best for baby, *best for baby*, best for baby.
I have done what is best for baby!!!"
SUKI, CIRENCESTER

Shit, I Need Some Mum Friends

WHEN HENRY WAS born I didn't have much of a friend network. My school/uni/work friends were yet to birth any babies (the carefree bastards) and I was more than a hundred miles away from my sister, who, at the time, had "just the one." (I'm surprised I never punched anybody who used the phrase "just the one" before Jude joined the party—"just the one" was bloody hard work and, at times, that was one too many for me to cope with.) Even traveling up to see my bestie, who found out she was pregnant just five months after I did, required a four-hour car journey. Hardly "pop round for a cuppa" territory.

I couldn't risk being shipwrecked alone on Parent Island. From the moment I confirmed my pregnancy hunch by peeing on a stick prior to jetting off to that shitty Kos hotel (I'm scowling if you're reading this, James), I knew I'd have to make new friends. The prospect of making "mummy friends" filled me with dread. I have always felt intimidated by large groups of girls, and at work I naturally formed my strongest bonds with male colleagues. So, aside from my school- and uni-friend gems, most of the new friends I had made in my early twenties were male. Superb for nights out and banter and chats about online-dating woes (theirs, not mine). Not so great for chats about episiotomy stitches and nipple cream. Shit. I was having a baby and needed to find me some mum friends. Where should I look?

I'd heard that one of the best ways of finding a Mummy Wolf Pack was by signing up for NCT (National Childbirth Trust) classes. My sister had done it, and I'd read about the groups—you meet other mums-to-be with similar due dates at local classes and then regroup once all your babies have landed. Somewhere along the line there is a Facebook photo of all the babies lined up on a picnic mat with the caption "The NCT crew" (possibly accompanied by awkwardly crouching dads who have also been dragged along). It sounded just the ticket. I needed some NCT buddies in my life. But, alas, when the time came to sign up online, there wasn't a group in my local area. Bollocks and arse. No NCT?! This meant I would have to make pals the old-fashioned way. I would have to fly solo to some baby groups and hope somebody wanted to be my BMFF (Best Mummy Friend Forever). Our bog-standard (and free) antenatal classes were more functional than they were social. In addition to watching the doll-in-the-birth-canal demonstration we mostly passed around those giant salad-server-type forceps and chatted about maternity pads. We smiled kindly at the other parents, but there wasn't a list of e-mail addresses circulated and a "February babies reunion" scheduled at a local farm park. I was quite sure I'd never see those people again. I would instead have to make my own way to mum gatherings and ask people for contact details—which sounded much like professional networking events I'd been to, only with fewer skirt suits and more maternity leggings.

By the time baby Henry arrived, I was mentally prepped for this New Friends task. Four weeks in, when James had returned to work, I decided I would venture out to a few groups and take it from there. A baby group . . . a breastfeeding group . . . a "stay and play" session after baby clinic . . . hell, I'd try them *all*! There was nothing to lose. Anyway, I did it. After at least two hours of frantically getting ready to leave the house each time ("You better not have done another poo—*oh, for fuck's sake!*"), I went along to these groups with a smile (and the baby). At times, it was a little daunting. Particularly bursting through the double doors of the local town hall with the pram, parking it up and realizing people were already midconversation. Daunting that I would have to wade in through the sensory baby toys, plonk myself down next to somebody and hope to fit in. That, by and large, there would be no men there and I would have to dip my toe into the female-only environment of cups of tea and chats about painful milk letdowns, totally obliterating my comfort zone.

But I did it, and I'm bloody glad I did, because those groups were a godsend (and, one time, I genuinely needed a chat about painful milk letdowns). I didn't struggle to make small talk with these groups of mums, as I'd feared, because it's almost *impossible* to run out of conversation when you are accompanied by a small person. A baby is the *best prop ever*. Ask "How old is she now?" or "Have you had her weighed today?" and you've banked an hour of chatting about the birth and feeding and what percentile she's on in that little red book. You interact behind the comfort screen of your babies, laughing at their windy smiles and cursing their poo schedules. Hey presto, all of a sudden you've found another friendly face to stop and chat with in the local convenience store when you're out and about trying to get the baby to have that *goddamn nap*.

That hour of tea and sympathy outside the house was priceless and gave me the much-needed motivation to get dressed and not stay indoors watching *Homes Under the Hammer* for the fifth consecutive day. The other mums were all really *nice*. But I still hadn't sussed out how to take it to the next level. I needed to be braver. I needed to entrap some friends I could meet up with outside the organized breastfeeding cafés and baby-clinic sessions. Friends who would pop round for that quick cuppa. Friends I could text when it kicked off at three a.m. and I needed to hear somebody else say, "It's been a bit shit here, too." I needed emotional support above and beyond the weaning small talk.

As it happened, a chance meeting one evening on our (then) housing estate was a real turning point in my New Friends adventure. Said encounter stemmed from a bit of a dark place. By "dark place," I mean James had returned from work that evening to find me once again in tears, sniveling about *The Chase*. (To be fair, it was the only program I'd attempted to watch that day and, with Henry being a total arse, his screaming over the cash-builder round was the straw that broke the mummy camel's back.) I handed the baby over and stormed out of the back door. It was one of those moments where I wished I'd picked up something warmer to wear, but having just made a dramatic exit it would have looked a bit crap to pop an arm back round the door for my fleece. So I kept walking. And, eventually, after an hour angrily striding around the countryside, muttering, "I won't put up with this shit," I felt calmer and decided to head back to check on the boys.

Just a few hundred yards away from home I bumped into a girl I was sure I had seen both at the antenatal classes and in the waiting room of the midwife's clinic. She must have had her baby by now. She was putting out her recycling and looked more than a bit pissed off, so I pottered over. "How's it all going?" I asked her. I wish I could remember her exact response word for word, but I can't. However, it must have been something along the lines of "Pretty horrendous," "Awful" or "I've had just about enough," because I distinctly remember thinking, "Thank God for that!" Not thank God that she was having an awful time of it, but thank God that it wasn't just me. That somebody else was saying, "Jesus, what have we done?" The relief was overwhelming.

Perhaps I wasn't broken, after all. Perhaps there were others like me having a shit time of it, too. Perhaps I was *normal.* I felt like a weight had been lifted, like I had somehow shaken off the loneliness that had been making me feel lost and more than a little bit sad. I loved her instantly. We stood for a good few minutes describing all the ways our lives had gone down the pan, and it was such a release. We agreed we would meet up, not at a baby group but at one of our houses. I think it was my first agreed "playdate," and I remember the joy of suspecting I had found someone like-minded. That I would have some proper company. I returned to James and (a still-screaming)

Henry with the biggest smile I'd had on my face in weeks. I recorded *The Chase* after that.

Hundreds of playdates (and some quality moaning) later, the relief of opening up that friendship has never left me. We spent hours discussing the perils of no sleep and bonding over the fact that we both missed our prebaby lives. We dreamed of work nights out and beach holidays, and it was our safe space to admit that away from any judgmental glares. But by the time Jude came along we had moved away from the area (and ironically downsized from that dream family home we could no longer afford—expensive things, babies), so I could no longer drop in for cheese on toast (with ketchup) and a moan about the kids when they both refused to nap. (Oh, how I miss her, though we *are* still in touch.) It was back to square one, and I was once again tasked with making a new set of mum friends in a new area. FML.

Second time around, however, I felt more confident about the New Friends thing. I knew what I was looking for and I felt braver. I'd discovered I could manage the "Do you fancy a coffee sometime?" approach because, after a couple of chats at Bounce and Rhyme, I had usually ascertained whether or not I would get on with someone or other. It's not an exact science, but when I've said, "God, having a newborn is like torture, isn't it? Roll on, bedtime!" and been met with a puzzled frown, I've made an on-the-spot assumption that the mum I'm chatting to might not be the best fit for a park date. When she has replied, "They can be such sods," "I need a glass of wine" or, better still, "Do you fancy going out for a glass of wine?"—I've made an on-the-spot decision that the mum could be a friend for life.

I've met mums who are borderline professional in their diary management of playdates—mums who have an impressively large number of friends. My Mummy Wolf Pack is very modest in comparison, but I'm happy. The ones I have are keepers. It's true I originally flinched at the very thought of "mummy friends" and "playdates," but both have proved pretty essential to my survival these past few years. I'm quietly relieved that I now have a few close mum friends to my name who can talk to me about significant mum-related things like pelvic-floor issues and *doing it* (you know [whispers], *sex*). I once feared I would find those motherhood conversations as dull as dishwater. Turns out I love chatting about stretch marks and postpartum intercourse as much as the next person.

Power to the mummy friends.

"Sod the glowing faces of new mums splashed on mags and those discount codes for expensive shops you'll never shop in again: what mums need is a bit of 'Don't panic, you'll be fine, we're all giving it a go, and we *all* think we're shit at it.'"
ANNECY, HAMPSHIRE

Mum Appearances Can Be Deceptive

PART OF MY MUM Friends journey (I'm just embracing "journey" now) has been the realization that mum stereotypes are just that: stereotypes. My experiences of meeting and talking to hundreds of mums (both mums I've met in person and those I've met virtually, via the blog) have shown me just how narrow-minded I was before.

I remember, midway through my first pregnancy, I was out on an appointment and having a conversation with one of my customers about her sister, who'd recently had a baby. "She's one of those, you know [lowers voice], *earth mothers*," she told me. Despite having never met said customer's sister, I instantly felt that I knew the sort of mother she must be. An *earthy* one. That meant she'd be all cloth nappies and baby-led (organic) weaning and fair-trade clothes, right?

When Henry arrived and I plodded off to those baby groups for the first time, I almost *wanted* to discover some good old-fashioned stereotypes: Earth Mothers, Career Mums, Stay-at-Home Mums, Yummy Mummies who wear designer everything, Slummy Mummies who don't seem to care very much about anything. It's just easier if you can put people into boxes, isn't it? I didn't feel very earthy, I definitely didn't feel very yummy (but hoped I wasn't *entirely* slummy), so I just guessed it would be best to make a beeline for the other nonearthy, nonyummy, non-slummy parents waiting outside Monkey Music. You know, the *normal* ones. And that is what I did: I chatted to the mums (and dads) who I thought looked "normal."

I realize now that this makes me sound like a totally judgmental knobhead (and that would be a fair assessment), but I think *I* was anxious about being judged by the other mums. In my tired and self-protective emotional state, I assumed that anybody earthy, for example, would judge me, mainly for my reliance on disposable nappies and Ella's Kitchen strawberry pouches. It was much easier to pluck up the courage to chat to (and make friends with) the mums who looked a bit like me (i.e., slightly disheveled, with baby sick and/or Dairylea on their leggings—nearly always a promising start).

And it is true that occasionally the mum stereotypes of myth and legend will prove a *little* bit accurate. Times when, despite ignoring the stereotype warning sign and trying to find common ground, there just hasn't been any. Once I tried talking to a mum outside one of Henry's baby groups who was doing some crocheting (granted, not my cup of tea, but I decided to strike up a pre-baby-group convo, anyway). I nodded along to her chat about crochet patterns and the family's "totally organic" lifestyle and how she would never go back to work again or indeed drink alcohol again because she just felt that there was no need to do either now she was a mother. I remember quite clearly that she said "mother" and not "mum" and I wondered if I would ever describe myself as a "mother" in conversation. Said mother also told me she didn't much like prams, and there I was detailing how I'd never attempted crochet, didn't much care for the price of all things organic and couldn't wait to return to work (as I wheeled my pram in, daydreaming about the bottle of wine in the fridge . . .).

But—and it's a pretty big but—that's genuinely the *only* time I can remember thinking, "Well, this is awkward." Because, by and large, the snap judgments I have made about other mums based on just one or two snippets of information have been way off the mark.

Like the time I secretly labeled a mum I'd met a "Career Mum" (she was going back to work, full-time, to a very good job), and she later told me it was all about the money and their mortgage payments and that they were actually considering downsizing so she could take a hit on the salary and work fewer hours.

Or the time I secretly labeled a mum a "Happy-Staying-at-Home Mum" because she had no plans at all to return to work but who later explained that she simply couldn't pay for child-care costs on her low salary and she would, in fact, have liked nothing better than a part-time job.

Or the time I met a very "Yummy Mummy" (everything

seemed designer—seriously, everything—and she always looked immaculate) and I later discovered she lived at the dodgier end of town. Exactly where she lived was, of course, irrelevant, but it was wrong of me to assume at first glance that she was well-off and living in luxury. I'd pictured her doing the school run in a Range Rover Evoque. She didn't even drive.

Appearances can indeed be deceptive.

I know it's impossible not to do it, to subconsciously categorize other parents based on the limited information we have (their appearance, usually), but I do make a bloody big effort *not* to do this nowadays. Not just because I have since made friends with mums who the pre-parent me might otherwise have avoided (okay: definitely *would* have avoided), but also because, even if no long-term friendship blossoms, it just makes life more interesting. How boring would it be if we were all the same? Some of the most hilariously frank and candid chats I've had about motherhood have been with mums I could so easily have written off as being "not my type."

I recently had the pleasure of meeting another mum I totally *would* have written off from afar. The mum in question, Zion, had just finished writing *The Ultimate Guide to Green Parenting*, and it's safe to say that, prior to my conversation with her, I had never given any thought to how green I was as a parent. To be "green," we'd surely have to abide by the aforementioned earthy way of life, get rid of the TV and start worrying about parabens. There was no way *she and I would have anything in common.*

What I actually discovered when I met her for coffee was

some quite fascinating stuff about the health benefits and cost savings (hurrah!) of all things green. We chatted happily about our children and our shared love of being outdoors. I'd never even considered our daily park trips and walks into town as being particularly "green," but I suppose our love of escaping the house on foot makes us at least partially greenish.

It was naive of me to assume a self-labeled "Green Parent" would be in some way judging me for my crimes against greenness. The chat inspired me to take action (well, to fish James's discarded empty yogurt pots out of the bin and list a couple of baby items on local selling sites; items which, if I'm honest, I would previously have taken straight to the dump). It's unlikely I'll be ditching the TV or checking the ethical consumer rating of all my toiletries anytime soon (because I love watching *Catfish* and I like the smell of Pantene). But it's fine to dabble in green parenting if you fancy it. It's fine to dabble in earthiness, too. I try my best to dabble in yumminess every once in a while, and I've definitely experimented with slumminess.

I've started to doubt whether anybody belongs firmly in any one camp. Parenting is not like the general election—you don't have to pick a side.

In hindsight, I have been foolish to steer clear of certain "types" of mum. Foolish to try to mentally affiliate *myself* with a type. Having put quite a lot of thought into my own parenting classification since baby Henry arrived in 2012, I have mostly just concluded that I'm not any type at all, unless "That'll Do" is a recognized style of parenting. I've probably dipped into all the stereotypes at some point.

All hail the dabbling!
I still don't get the crochet thing, though.

"When my boy was about six months old I went out for dinner with my NCT group. I assumed everyone was thinking what I was thinking so I said it, the thing we must never say: 'It's a bit fucking boring, though, isn't it?' You could've heard a pin drop. Tumbleweed blew across the restaurant."

HELEN, CHESHIRE

My Babywearing Incompetence

"Have you tried babywearing?"

"Sorry?" Three months into motherhood and I still had that rabbit-in-the-headlights look whenever anybody asked me a baby-based question. This particular mum was being helpful—I had been complaining about my baby, who would not stop moaning unless he was in some way attached to my person, and she was offering a potential solution.

"You know, putting him in a sling or a wrap?"

Oh, *that*. I'd been calling it baby carrying, like a complete novice. I would soon discover that my limited knowledge of baby *carriers* (i.e., the ones with clips and buckles your parents had in the 1980s) did not even scratch the surface of this baby-wearing movement I would be introduced to. A whole new world of woven wraps and infant slings and back carrying I never knew existed opened up to me. It's not just about sticking the baby in a BabyBjörn and heading out for a quick dog walk anymore. *Hell no.* There are babywearing websites, and organized sling meets, and Facebook pages for sharing babywearing tips and accessories. Mind = blown.

Having received advice from some very kind mum friends, including my stepsister, who is a babywearing *pro*, I purchased my first wrap. I say "wrap," but what I actually purchased was a piece of material not too dissimilar from one of those fabrics aerial gymnasts hang off. I'm not shitting you, it was at least three hundred yards long. I remember thinking, "What the hell have I taken on?" as it unraveled.

But I had it covered. I'd witnessed mums using these slings and wraps before, and on one occasion two proficient babywearers had even given me an impromptu intervention (wrapping me up in one of their wraps). It looked pretty simple. Something about finding the middle of the material and making sure the edges weren't twisted. Over one shoulder . . . over the other . . . the slack could be adjusted before something got tucked somewhere . . . how hard could it be?

It probably isn't hard. But I was clueless. By the time it arrived I'd forgotten everything from that informal lesson, and when it came to our first babywearing trial I resorted to the font of all knowledge that is YouTube. I vividly remember standing in my kitchen one evening with the iPad propped up on the worktop, watching a video of a very calm woman using a doll to demonstrate the ease of a simple FWCC (that's a front wrap cross carry to you and me). I tried following her steps in real time, but as I stood there, getting sweatier by the minute and entangled in sling material, I changed tactics and started pausing the video at crucial moments. Finally, I'd done it and braved positioning a slightly startled Henry in the wrap I hoped was the perfect imitation of the woman's in the YouTube clip. I called James in to assess my achievement. "Ta-dah! Does it look like hers does from the back?" I asked him. He looked at the paused video on the iPad and the woman's neatly wrapped pretend baby and then back at Henry, who was housed in what can only be described as a baggy mess of material. The woman's "baby" was snugly tucked in against her chest, with just the optimum amount of slack. Mine was slacker than a slack sack (100 percent still talking about the wrap), and Henry was suspended awkwardly somewhere around my belly button, crying. I took a deep breath in, removed the baby, put the video back to the beginning and begged James to help. We'd tackle this bastard wrap together. *Let's be having you.* It wasn't the most exciting video we'd ever watched together (steady), and the pair of us attempting to wrap a crying baby that evening in the kitchen was one of our earliest "How the fuck did this become our life?" moments.

My babywearing incompetence was so ridiculous it should have been funny. LOL and at least one ROFL. But I wasn't laughing. I had sweat patches. In fact, I got so agitated and flustered that the YouTube kitchen master class culminated in me crying (standard) and attempting to throw the *"piece-of-shit stupid wrap"* on the floor. (I didn't even manage that convincingly, because I was still tangled up in the bloody thing. *Grrrrrrr.*) My armpits feel hot just thinking about it.

Some weeks later, I cracked it. Well, I cracked getting Henry into the wrap, provided I had twenty minutes to spare and was standing in front of a mirror. I still looked like a sweaty octopus as I launched the material over my shoulders, but I got better at adjusting the slack. It was initially a bit of a revelation, to be honest: free hands, no cumbersome pram crashing into shop doorways, a squishy little face free to vomit down my bra without anybody noticing.

But I never got any better at the unwrapping and rewrapping when out and about and under pressure. I just wasn't skillful enough. I used to find myself leaving coffee shops with a partially wrapped baby and achy shoulders. Or standing by the boot of my car, having parked up somewhere, attempting to adjust the all-important slack and ending up in a state of sweaty distress. They should add wrapping baby slings to the Sure "It won't let you down" advert.

So my babywearing career was a short one. I later dabbled in a few further slings/wraps/carriers, including a side-carrying contraption and a fabric crossover one which fastened with Velcro, but I fell out with and swore at them all. I still look wistfully at other babywearing mums and dads (as I crash the pram into somebody else's ankles outside TK Maxx) and think, "I need to revisit this," but after our most recent attempt (an expensive clippy contraption that Jude hates—he tries to beat the shit out of my breastbone whenever he is in it) I think I'm done. I'm told no single babywearing option fits all, and I'm sure there is a suitable alternative out there for me. Perhaps I just haven't found the One. Perhaps I should burst out of the comfort zone and drop into a local sling meet for advice on trying pocket wrap cross carrying. Perhaps I've never recovered from the crushing sense of failure experienced during YouTube Kitchen Wrap–Gate.

More than likely, I just can't be arsed.

Part Two

LIFE, BUT NOT AS WE KNEW IT

"I misplaced a breast pad
in the ball pool once."

Your Day Versus His Day: Why Nobody Is Winning

WHEN MORNING COMES around, I sometimes look at the day stretching out in front of me and think, "Oh, God." James's alarm goes off and he gets up, has a shower and gets ready for work. My alarm these days is Henry, who loudly shouts, "Are you awake, Mummy? My pajama bottoms are wet. I can't find my fire engine. Can I have some Weetos?" If I'm particularly lucky, a series of recorded Minion farts will be the first thing I hear when I wake up, as the fart blaster from *Despicable Me 2* is activated next to my head, waking Jude, who promptly performs his first dump of the day. FML. And so the morning circus begins . . .

"Have a good day," I sneer at my husband as he leaves the house. On time. Without juggling a car-seat-and-pram-base combo into the car. Without worrying if he's got enough baby wipes and a clean muslin that doesn't smell of cheese. Occasionally, listening to *actual* music on an iPod. Bastard.

Back in the land of the living room, at least one half of my offspring is kicking off and I am left wondering whether 8:35 is too early for *Toy Story 3*, or whether I should wait to see what's coming up on *Lorraine* instead . . . And, more to the point, I'm left pondering the same daily conundrum: what the actual fuck am I going to do with them all day?

"You don't appreciate how lucky you are, going to work," I tell him. "I wish we could swap." Maternity leave housed the worst of this resentment, but even after returning to work part-time, my two days "off" (*grrrr*) often prompted some spiteful comparisons and I still find myself getting proper mardy toward my full-time-working spouse. In theory, this part-time pattern is only temporary, to see us through the baby years, but I'm four years in now and it doesn't feel all that temporary. My weekday pattern has morphed into something unrecognizable from just a few years ago, and his has not. This irritates me. The problem is, I know it irritates him, too, because the flip side is he's working his arse off five days a week and I'm spending two days at home with our lovely boys.

"I'd happily swap!" he tells me. "I'd *love* to work three days a week." He isn't being spiteful or provocative when he says this—he genuinely likes the idea of a part-time workweek.

"Ha! You have absolutely *no idea*!" I scoff. And on it rumbles . . .

Well, I have come to realize that an ongoing "my day is harder than your day" debate is ridiculous. And pointless. It doesn't make either of you feel any better and it's largely unfair to all concerned.

When I was on maternity leave for the second time, I began to grasp that my jealousy about his freedom to leave the house had been somewhat ill informed by the memory of what working life was like *before* we had children. Work may well be like a holiday at times (see "SAHMs, I Salute You," page 149)—and I bloody love working—but it is still *work*. And, with a baby plus threenager at home, James has to get through his working day on significantly less sleep. Then, after work, when his shift is finished, he doesn't return to a tidy, quiet house, put on Sky Sports News and have a cold beer, like he sometimes used to when I was working late at the bank. He comes home to me. Stressed. Me sitting scowling amidst mountains of shitty plastic toys and possibly a shitty nappy. Telling him how much I hate being at home. How much I hate my life (the dramatic license of arguments!). Telling him I am at breaking point and no, I don't know what is for fucking tea because *I haven't even had a shower*. At times, I would simply show him a video recorded earlier in the day of one or both of the children screaming and comment: "My whole day." I'm surprised he didn't sign up for an additional evening job.

I think the penny has now dropped that I need to curb this almost boastful "my day was worse than yours" carry-on. I've never really achieved anything by giving my husband shit when he comes through the door. Every now and again, I just feel hard done by and want recognition that I have drawn the short straw. I want him to get out his ruler and confirm that my straw is shorter. I need him to *get* it. But, equally, he is fed up with hearing my persistent whining and wants to remind me that he has been at work all day ("Well, *lucky* you . . ." And on it goes . . .).

The thing is, on reflection, I know I have been a bit unfair. It is true that on my home days he does "escape" at 8:25. And he can listen to music on the iPod (though he's dicing with the risk of "Let It Go" and/or "Hakuna Matata" on shuffle). It is true that I am sometimes bored to tears by 9:25—I can't cope with *Jeremy Kyle* anymore; I struggle to get past the lack of teeth and the fact that two toothless people had sex but seem surprised it resulted in a baby, who they've named Mercedes-Leigh.

It is true that there are, genuinely, many days I *would* rather be at work.

But none of this proves that my husband is "winning." I'm sure he really does wake up some Monday mornings, look at the week stretching out in front of him and think, "I wish I could stay at home." His jealousy of me is just as valid as mine is of him. But all he gets is me dismissing his feelings as ridiculous, telling him how hard it is at home and reiterating that he has *no idea*. I'm not exactly wrong in that assertion—he doesn't have any idea what being at home with two kids under three all day every day for months on end is like. He has never had to do it. But that's not really his fault. By the same token, I don't really know what working full-time and coming home to Hurricane Wife (and surrounding devastation) is like either. In the hardest of my maternity-leave months I often forgot even to ask how his day had been. It might have been awful. I was too busy instantly offloading the full breakdown of the reasons my day had been horrific, reasons my day had been ten times harder than his, reasons he had already heard in abusive, sweary texts sent earlier in the day. Texts like:

- I'd rather be a bin lady than deal with this shit.
- Don't phone me at lunch. I've got nothing nice to say.
- Where are you? Text me the moment you leave. You need to pick up nappies—I couldn't even get to the shop because they've done nothing but play up like twats *all* day.
- *You better not be late. I've fucking had enough of your kids.*

These are actual texts (not proud).

I text when I feel compelled to text, which, unfortunately, tends to be when I have gone off on one. Such messages aren't a balanced view of the situation at all—I have plenty of great days, just me and the boys hanging out, that never make the text-message edit, bar the odd token WhatsApp picture of them on a steam train. Sure, I moan about my days "off"—the midweek ones, especially. But even for die-hard work fans there are benefits to being at home. *Sometimes*, it is the better deal. On top of the summer sun and catching up with friends and extra cuddles (the nonsnotty ones), there is something undeniably liberating about being master of your own schedule on the days you are not at work. If you choose to, you can simply decide at two p.m. on a Tuesday that you fancy a trip to the library. And go. Admittedly, you won't get there until four p.m. because it is impossible to leave the sodding house in less than ninety minutes . . . But, to a certain extent, you decide what you do with your time. It's the kids who roll the behavior dice and decide how successful that outing is. You still answer to *somebody*, but the boss or bosses breathing down your neck are much smaller. And can be bribed with raisins.

I feel I should add at this point that what I am writing is based purely on the dynamic in our household. This isn't a sweeping generalization that the mum of the household is at home on kids duty more than the dad is—this is often not the case. It might be the other way around. You might be in a same-sex marriage where it is not "her versus him" at all. You might both work full-time. You might both work part-time. You might be a single parent.

Hats off to you all.

But if you share our dynamic, perhaps the grass really *isn't* greener on the work side. Some days, it is. Some days, it isn't. Some days, one of you has a distinct advantage. Some days, you both lose. The only certainty is that, unless you are genuinely considering addressing the work/home divide (and reallocating roles), the constant "my day has been shittier than yours" debate could roll on forever, which doesn't help anyone. What has so far proved more helpful is to crack open a bottle of wine on Friday night and agree you've both had a hard week. This promotes a feeling of solidarity—and there's wine. Everybody wins.

Important Notes for the Worker

- If the baby is teething or if anybody at home is ill you *definitely* have the better deal being at work.

- Don't pretend you have any idea what it is like to take a crying baby to the doctor's for injections accompanied by a toddler who has switched to arsehole mode. Truly, she has lived through hell that day.
- If she is having a "moment," cut her some slack. She doesn't really hate you. Or the kids. Or the house. Or her life. But she is at a (temporary) breaking point. Those abusive, sweary text messages aren't her new hobby, but sometimes she can't stop herself. Sometimes, she doesn't know what else to do. Don't sigh. In fact, on those days, it's sometimes best not to even breathe near her. It's nothing personal, but she might want to smack you in the face.
- Finally, never, *ever* ask what she has been doing all day. Or if your work shirts have been washed. She hasn't even washed herself. You know where the washing machine is.

And for Those Holding the Fort at Home . . .

I know it's bloody annoying when he says, "But I've been at work all day!" but he has been at work. *All day.* And he never, ever gets to sunbathe during toddler nap time. Or watch *Loose Women* in his pj's on a Thursday. Or meet a friend for coffee and cake. Just admit it: there are some small perks. Although, James, if you're reading this, I know how hard you work, but I think we could just agree that being at home is a *teeny tiny* bit harder and that buying wine and/or making me a cup of tea is the least you can do. In return, I'll try to stop giving you shit via text message.

"I'm so glad my little boy waited until you could hear a pin drop at the library before asking, 'Why has that lady got a beard?'"

KELLY, NORFOLK

Let's Talk About Sex, Baby

[ABSOLUTELY NO NEED for you to read this chapter, Dad—or my future teenage sons, for that matter.]

"Are we having sex tonight?" Transparent questioning from James.

"Err, I dunno. Are we agreeing sex in advance nowadays?"

"No, I just wondered if I should Sky Plus some of my programs."

"Right, well, I don't know."

"That's a no, then?"

"It's probably a no."

"Okay. In that case, I don't need to record *Wheeler Dealers*. Cuppa?"

There are no two ways about it: having children changes your relationship. Sometimes for the better, sometimes for the worse and, sadly, sometimes for*ever* to the point of collapse.

(When I blogged about the post-having-children relationship dynamic, I received several "My post-having-children relationship dynamic was *divorce*!" comments, which, though offered in jest, did seem to prompt an assortment of "Me, too, the bastard!"–type replies . . .)

For many of us, I think the relationship is just *different*. Despite my crazed and irrational meltdowns, James and I continue to get on like a house on fire. I'm not one to plaster "Love you, baby—you're my rock, my soul mate—*you complete me*" all over Facebook (because I could, you know, just *tell* him that), but I have realized while writing this book just how fortunate I am to have married such a good egg. Throughout all the disastrous toddler mealtimes and the sleepless nights and all the other shit (sometimes actual shit, sometimes the shit that is on the floor), we often find ourselves crying with laughter or enjoying a moment in the kitchen when we dance to songs on the radio while doing the dishes. (God bless Heart FM for churning out songs like N-Trance's "Set You Free" and Charles & Eddie's "Would I Lie to You?" Absolute classics.)

It's true I moan about the kids a lot; I know I do. I moan because at times it's just all so bloody hard, isn't it? (Have I said that yet?) But how *we* are, how our marriage is, what having kids has "done to us" is genuinely not something I need to grumble about. We're all good.

Nevertheless, the boys have brought with them some changes to our relationship, and I reckon we're not alone.

Doing It

I'm just putting it out there that I suspect a decline in the frequency of having sex is symptomatic not only of becoming parents but also more generally of being married or having been together for a number of years (nine for us, by the time Henry arrived). Life is busy. Discounting the first year of our relationship, holidays abroad and the spells we were trying for a baby, we weren't exactly at it like rabbits before the children came along. Without having any tangible idea of what constitutes a "normal" sex life, I'd hazard a guess that we're somewhere on that normal spectrum.

Sometimes, we have sex.

Sometimes, we are too busy or too tired (okay: *I* am too busy or too tired).

Sometimes, I would quite honestly rather sit in my dressing gown watching *Broadchurch.*

Adding children to the mix was never going to tip the balance back in favor of getting down to it more often, but it is what it is. I can't comment on having sex in the first few months after giving birth because, quite frankly, I wouldn't know; there was nothing about soggy breast pads and larger-than-normal knickers that made me want sex in those early days, and if I had half an hour to lie down I wanted sleep and nothing more. I have heard from other mums who "got intimate" within a few weeks of childbirth, and that's great; I simply found it too hard to disassociate *down there* from stitches and placenta retrieval for at least a couple of months. (And maybe by a couple I mean six.)

Even now that some normality has resumed, I think it's fair to say that sex is rarely at the top of the agenda; certainly, the majority of messages via social media and conversations I've had face-to-face have reinforced this point. They've also reminded me of the comedy moments that having sex as a parent can deliver, such as:

- Attempting to have some nookie while the baby naps, only to hear him cooing and gurgling from the next room. "Mama, Mama, Mama, bottle bot bot!" = mood ruined.
- The equally moment-killing threat of a toddler or small child pottering in and discovering Mummy and Daddy "wrestling." Even worse is having to stop just as you reach the "point of no return" because you think someone's out of bed. (Cheers, Jason, via Twitter, for sharing this particular scenario—I couldn't help but picture your state of imminent euphoria crossed with moderate panic, which, let's face it, can't be healthy for anyone.)
- Genuinely deciding whether "tonight's the night" (or not) as you do the supermarket shop. ("Are we having any action later? Do you know if we're out of pita breads?") We 100 percent do this; it's better to know where you stand so you can judge whether you need to bother with a shower and/or tape *Gogglebox*, right? Spontaneity is dead to us.
- The times sheer exhaustion takes over and you:

  - Both fall asleep despite best-laid plans.
  - Downgrade the act of lovemaking to something speedier (you *know* the one).

- Quite like the idea but can't be bothered to make any real effort so both partially keep your pajamas on. I'm pretty sure the Comfy Pajama Quickie never featured in *More* magazine's "Position of the Fortnight" feature, but parents of small children can't be aspiring to the reverse cowgirl and three orgasms in one session, can they? *Can they?*

- Having to do the postsex loo dash (you *know* the one) in absolute silence for fear of waking the children.
- Remembering with childish giggles the times you got jiggy in places other than your bed/occasionally on the sofa (like that time in the changing room . . . *Stop reading, Dad*).

Time as a Couple

It's not just sexy time (*ha*) that takes a hit. Once the offspring have landed, quality time of *any* sort becomes largely nonexistent, doesn't it? Sometimes, the most loving of acts in our house is for one of us to facilitate five minutes' peace for the other by taking over child-care duties. If I want to savor a shower (or a wee) in peace or, on the rarest of occasions, stay in bed past six thirty a.m., James must entertain the small ones.

Occasionally, he says, "Why don't you have a nap, babe?" and I look at him like he has handed over a winning lottery ticket or bought me a Terry's Chocolate Orange. So much love right there. With small children at large, there is no commodity more valuable than sleep, and on the days I'm flying solo with the boys I'd genuinely be prepared to start giving away our household appliances in exchange for a nap. I suspect I am not alone in this uninterrupted-nap fantasy.

Likewise, if James wants to watch even one half of a football match without Henry smacking him around the head with a lightsaber and/or noise interference from the VTech baby walker ("Welcome to our learning farm; we have lots to show you"—Piss *off*), I must vacate the living room and take the tiny terrors with me. I know we've got a good thing going on with our unspoken agreement to offer each other a break, but it's like shift work. We never get to have a break *together*.

And what happens when you finally *do* find yourselves gloriously child free, maybe at a nice restaurant? Well, if you're anything like us you will eat your posh meals in thirty seconds flat (subconsciously trained to expect the mealtime meltdown) and spend the entire evening talking about . . . the kids.

"Isn't it cute when you tell Jude not to climb up on his pram and he knows he's being naughty so he gives you that cheeky smile?"

"Did I send you that picture of Henry in the sandpit? Hang on, I'll find it and WhatsApp it to you . . ."

And we realize we have become more than a bit obsessed with our monsters and miss them dearly, so happily settle the bill and go home to check on them sleeping. And then have an early night ourselves.

A fully covered pajama night, usually.

Slack Pelvic Floor and Empty Boobs

I DEFINITELY UNDERESTIMATED the impact that growing and birthing small people would have on my body—those interesting physical developments that can strike both in pregnancy and postbirth. By "postbirth," I fear I may mean forever, because some of the changes I've experienced are highly unlikely to be reversed without a trip to Harley Street.

I always find any mention of "postbaby body hang-ups" really grating, so I give the "Celeb Mum Loses Mum Tum in Just 7 Days!" front covers the one-fingered salute while muttering, "Oh, fuck right off!" whenever I'm in Tesco. I certainly didn't lose my "mum tum" in seven days (it took me the best part of a year to level out at my prebaby weight), but I suppose I haven't fared too badly at "shedding those pregnancy pounds" (*grrrr*), if you discount the fact that I'm still wearing Mothercare

M2B pajama bottoms I purchased during my first pregnancy, mainly for comfort reasons on days I find myself pregnant with a Galaxy Minstrels baby.

But postbirth body changes are not all about weight loss; and, to be honest, weight, as in actual pounds of flesh, is probably where the similarities between my pre- and postbaby body start and end. I get told, "You've got your figure back!" and, "You wouldn't even know you've had children!" quite a lot, which is really flattering, but these people *haven't seen me naked*. They haven't shared a car journey with me and had to stop four times because I'm going to piss myself. My body knows I've had children. Trust me: *it knows*. Hidden beneath those jeans from *before* (high five!), the signs are all there.

That said, I've heard from women who've experienced pretty major complications following childbirth, so I count myself bloody lucky to be functioning normally. I therefore don't class my physical developments as "hang-ups" at all and have in fact started to accept them simply as changes—changes which, unsurprisingly, resulted from growing half a stone of human, then pushing it out of my vagina (twice).

So my postbaby body observations are just that: observations about my own body. I hope I never bump into any of you—*ever*—and if I do, let's just agree we'll all pointedly forget I've shared far too much information. Here we go . . .

My Boobs Have Gone

Henry and Jude basically ate my boobs. It is a bit of a shame as, when I was pregnant and breastfeeding, I had a reasonable cleavage even *without* my bra on. I kind of wish I'd taken some pictures or got one of those godawful DIY belly-and-boob casting kits. (Christ, I'm really sorry if you have a cast of your pregnant belly and boobs hanging in your hallway next to a giant canvas of your heads from your wedding; it's just not my cup of tea. But I digress.)

Anyway, my Pamela Anderson boobs were short-lived and, at present, I'm quietly confident I could fit my tiny, empty sacks into the 28AA trainer bra from my prepubescent years. "More than a handful's a waste," apparently, which is just as well— you'd fit *both* of mine in one hand.

I'm not overly bothered, actually. No real issues about having tiny man pecs. Though I really do need to go and get myself measured and buy myself some new bras, because you could, quite honestly, house small family pets in the vacant spaces in my bra cups.

So long, ample C-cup breasts, you served me well.

I Can't Hold It

My wee, I mean. I used to pride myself on my ability to "hold it in." On those long motorway journeys in heaving holiday traffic I would say, "Don't worry about stopping yet; let's at least get on the M4." The "Next Services: 30 Miles" sign would have been plenty of notice. I may even have continued to sip water as we approached the stop, safe in the knowledge that bladder relief was imminent. One time, I traveled for eight hours in the car without the urge for a wee and I *never* needed a wee during the night. I was pretty hard-core at bladder control.

I do slightly mourn those days.

I was okay(ish) after having Henry, but since having Jude it's safe to say the old pelvic floor has been challenged. I think said floor works at around 50 percent capacity, and there are days I wonder if it's even still there at all. I was lazy at doing my pelvic-floor exercises: "Do them for half an hour while watching *Coronation Street*," somebody told me once, and I did *try*, but I was forever distracted (pelvic floor . . . pelvic floor . . . "Oh, I don't like Gail's shirt, do you?").

I should have exercised harder. If you're reading this and you're pregnant, *do some now*. The challenge is to do them without making a nonchalantly casual face like when you're peeing in the sea (or, you know, how I *imagine* one might look if one were peeing in the sea . . .). Just take it from me, the shit they scare you with about bladder weakness is real; and nowadays, when I need to go, I *need to go* and, while there's no requirement for Tena Lady yet, every so often, when I don't get to the loo quick sharp, a little bit comes out. Sometimes that happens when I race Henry to the park. Or run up the stairs with any kind of bounce. PMSL is a genuine threat.

Things Down There

Pelvic-floor failings aside, things "down below" are all right, but they're not the same. Come on, they're just not. You hear horror stories about third-degree tears and stitches and prolapses (genuinely, the latter makes me feel quite faint), so, once again, I feel I have been let off easy, but we all have a fanny tale to tell and I'm no exception.

"It's so much better to have stitches—it's a lot tidier," somebody once remarked. "Tidier" it may be, but I'll be honest with you, whoever stitched me up the first time was aiming less for "as it was before" and more "virgin bride." You probably don't need to know this. Do you want to know this? Oh, sod it, I'm just sharing that this can happen because I, for one, certainly never expected to have a tightness problem postbaby. (It was later confirmed said seamstress had indeed got a bit needle-and-thread happy.) I had no stitches after Jude, and I'm not sure if that was the right decision. I can remember the midwife commenting that I "could use a few stitches," but I think we all got a bit distracted by that attention-seeking placenta and forgot.

So now I'm left with something that loosely resembles the original, if you get my drift. I'd rate it seven out of ten. Much like the shrunken boobs, it is what it is.

Stretch Marks

I was quietly relieved when I didn't get any stretch marks with Henry. After succumbing to advertising campaigns about stretch-mark prevention I had Bio-Oiled myself up religiously throughout the pregnancy. Second time around, I didn't have the time, the inclination or the toiletries budget to oil up my boobs and bump so I reckon I halfheartedly massaged in some baby oil once or twice at best. Maybe I'm a walking controlled experiment for Bio-Oil usage as, sure enough, stretch marks arrived at the very end of pregnancy two, but I strongly suspect it was less my lack of massage and more Jude's one-week extra stay in the utero hotel (and subsequent extra pound of weight) that prompted those purple, threadlike fuckers to show up. Mostly on my hips and inner thighs. *My thighs!* Why my thighs grew so much in pregnancy I'll never know, but they did, and those now-silvery inner-thigh squiggles are the most visible pregnancy legacies I have (other than the children, obviously).

I have seen some wonderful social-media campaigns all about empowering women to feel confident about their "mummy bodies," and I think these are really important. They fly in the face of the "beach body ready" advertising campaigns and make me want to high-five everybody involved. But I never feel *quite* empowered enough to share those "I'm a god-damn mummy tiger who earned her stripes!"–type stretch-mark pictures on Facebook because, at the end of the day, if we're cutting out the bullshit, I'd quite honestly prefer not to be stripy.

Overall Wellness

I was at least partially prepared for most of the aforementioned body quirks. No major surprises, except the genuine risk of wetting myself on a bouncy castle, which I thought was an urban legend.

The thing I probably underestimated most of all was the impact that having kids would have on my overall health. I'm not talking about my mental health (which undoubtedly suffered in the earliest months) but about feeling a bit ropy physically.

A bit ropy *all of the time*.

If I counted the days in each of my baby's first years when I wasn't feeling 100 percent, I would get to at least 364. It always amazes me how little recovery time you get as a new mum, and I'm sure that plays a part. Whichever way the baby comes out—C-section, forceps, in the giant bloody bath—I'm sure that days later you still feel like you have been involved in a major traffic accident with an Eddie Stobart lorry.

And yet you just get on with it, even though you've been thrown in at the deep end with nothing but a Bounty pack. Months later, after an average of 3.2 hours' sleep a night, I think it all catches up with you and comes out as colds and sore throats. Nobody warned me about the not-feeling-100-percent, feeling-more-like-60-percent-at-all-times-except-when-you've-had-a-gin-and-tonic effect of having children.

In fact, even if they had warned me, I would have just thought, "Nah, not me! I'll be different."

So maybe that was for the best. Though I do wish I'd taken the pelvic-floor exercising seriously.

"I took motherhood so seriously in the early years
and as a result had a very unhappy time of it.
I've since discovered that laughter is
the best medicine."
ALEX, DORKING

Nights Out:
The Baby Years

Ah, the GBNO (Great British Night Out). An institution of hair straightening and Lambrini swigging, followed by pubs, a club, a greasy kebab and the promise of doing bugger all the next day apart from drinking Coke and eating salt-and-vinegar crisps in bed.

It's way too depressing to conclude that this *all* has to change when we become parents, but it's impossible to deny that an evening out is much rarer these days. When the opportunity does present itself, the GBMNO (Great British Mum Night Out) is *slightly* different from the consequence-free, alcohol-inhaling carnage of yesteryear.

Back in the day, I used to spend the best part of a day getting ready for a night out. On occasion, if I had a proper event to go to, like a party or a wedding, preparations started the day *before*.

This prep might have included preening activities such as nail painting, exfoliation or fake-tan application. Sometimes, on a Saturday, it might even have involved a late-afternoon nap followed by a long bath and some bacon sarnies to line my stomach.

During the glory days (*c.* 2003–2011), a big night out with the girls used to be just as much about the getting ready (and getting hammered via the dangerously misleading strength of homemade cocktails) as it was about the time spent actually *out*. Once we had all piled into one of our bedrooms, the drinks would flow, the hair straighteners and perfume would be out in force and Kiss FM or *Huge Hits 2005* would provide the soundtrack to our leisurely makeup application. We'd discuss texts from boys and swap beautifying tips—there were no YouTube contouring tutorials back then; you basically just shoveled on bronzer and teamed it with the lip gloss you'd bought from Superdrug earlier that day. I can remember occasions when I got 100 percent ready and then at the last minute decided to change into something else and/or redo my hair. Just for fun.

Because I could.

Right now, this seems ludicrous. I almost want to smack the pre-parent me in the face: a face fresh from sleep, a face which said, "I just can't decide which skimpy outfit to wear, but no dramas because whichever one I *don't* choose can be road-tested next week when I do this all over again!"*

---

*In the glory days, I had no regard for the "legs or cleavage" rule so it was, in fact, very often, all out. With that in mind, I'm retracting the smack in the face and high-fiving the pre-parent me instead. The pre-parent me was badass. I love her and miss her every day.

Fast-forward to nowadays, and there is no substantial prep. No afternoon nap (pah!). No hot soak in the bath. No trip to Superdrug to buy a new lip gloss. No face mask. No hair mask (yes, I used to do these). No walking around in a post-fake-tan starfish, attempting to avoid the orange armpit line of doom. Nowadays, I rush a shower as Henry shouts, "Mummy? Mummy? Can I have a biscuit? Can you put *Scooby-Doo* on? Luke Skywalker's trousers have fallen off! Mummy. Mummy? *Mummy!*" from the living room while Jude pushes against the shower door and tries to grab my ankles.

I haven't exfoliated in years (I'm probably carrying around a load of dead skin and would be half a stone lighter if I set to work with some of those shower mitts), and my last attempt at fake-tan application was cut short by the urgency of Henry's daily poo. I ended up with a "tan" that started at my collarbone and finished at my knees.

"Making an effort" on a standard day involves throwing on a jazzy scarf over my trusty jeans-and-jumper combo and straightening the front third of my hair, which I do in thirty seconds flat and with a baby hanging off one leg. Those are the days I am *winning*. Other days, I wipe vomit crust from my leggings with a baby wipe and later return from the drugstore to find I left the house with toothpaste on my chin or Weetos in my teeth. (I *know* they are a children's cereal, and an unhealthy one at that. I don't want to hear it.)

So what *does* become of the Badly Tanned Me on the rare occasions I am invited out somewhere for the evening? Invited out on the promise of conversing with grown-up people, the promise of drinking wine, the promise of dancing around with an actual proper handbag like a clutch (*a clutch!*) and not a pram bag filled to the brim with bum-changing paraphernalia?

For starters, getting out of the house is Mission Impossible. After tackling the bedtime pandemonium (and strategically skipping every other page of *The Gruffalo's Child* because I'm already half an hour behind the getting-my-arse-out-of-the-door target time), I have to find something to wear. On my first evening out after Jude was born (a proper social outing, I mean, not nipping to Matalan to look at cot bedding), I made the mistake of trying on potential outfits at the last minute.

Bloody hell.

Even if you think you're doing quite well postbaby, nothing screams *"Wobbly!"* quite like squeezing your slightly engorged breasts and their unattractive nursing-bra container into a going-out dress from days gone by. On the evening in question, this situation was made all the more problematic because young Jude (around five months at the time) was still sleeping in our bedroom and I therefore had to rummage around quietly in the dark for potential going-out clobber.

So I didn't feel prepped or glam but, after very nearly throwing an "I look like a sack of shit—I'm not going" hissy fit, I decided that, ultimately, it didn't matter. What did matter was that I was within touching distance of letting my hair down and spending an evening *not* watching an ITV drama starring Suranne Jones (though, credit where credit's due, she is great at dramas). I decided to throw on something resembling a dressy top and some skinny(ish) jeans freshly Febrezed from an earlier wear in the week. I wouldn't let my high spirits about escaping the house be dampened by a slightly uninspiring outfit. I dug out some jewelry, located a pair of heels in the downstairs "messy cupboard," packed a lip gloss (probably one I'd purchased from Superdrug in 2005) and, one hour later, I was in a bar, listening to actual music not sung by Justin Fletcher, drinking gin and chatting with friends. I was *out*.

I have subsequently managed a few nights out with more successful outfit planning—this has become easier as the babies have grown bigger. I should tell you, though, that a *jumpsuit* is not a good outfit choice if the post-baby-bearing you needs a wee all the time. I spent half of one night out practically getting naked to go to the loo. What was I thinking? Usually, I'm just grateful to be wearing something that isn't covered in Sudocrem or sour milk and chatting about something *normal*—you know, like the fact that music has become "just noise" and that you need a second mortgage to afford a cocktail.

These days, a "night out" is just that. It is a well-deserved night *out of the house*. A well-deserved night away from the feeding and the sterilizing and the simultaneous watching of the telly and Facebook refreshing. As long as my outfit is sick free and I have some makeup in my bag, I will be winning as soon as I leave the house . . .

. . . and losing at 5:15 a.m., when the euphoria of having escaped the daily grind and downing some Prosecco with people much cooler than me has well and truly worn off. When, after four hours' sleep, I wake up with that fuzzy-mouthed, heavy-headed nausea to a declaration from my toddler that he needs a poo and I realize that there will be no salt-and-vinegar crisps and Coke in bed because I've agreed to go to a soft-play party and supervise the Passing of the Bloody Parcel.

More than anything else, the worst bit about nights out when you are the owner of small people is the consequence of your short-lived freedom the next day.

The show must go on.

If only the night-out freedom lasted until brunch, eh?

Soft-Play Hellholes

SOFT PLAY is love/hate for parents. Sometimes both at the same time. After my initial pained expression at the first-ever mention of a "soft-play date" (*Somebody make it stop!*), I've grown quite fond of these places. And that is saying something. If you have no idea what I'm talking about, picture a huge room, usually windowless and on an industrial estate, filled with floor-to-ceiling squashy play equipment and slides. Usually named something like Jungle Juniors or the Krazy Kidzone (yes, that's "crazy" with a "k"—absolutely scandalous), they are hot spots for parents to meet up and let those Krazy Kidz run riot. *Why?* you may be asking. Just *why?* Well, soft-play establishments may sound like Dante's Inferno, but they go hand in hand with the promise of catching up with friends and banking enough physical activity to safeguard a toddler nap in time for *Murder,*

She Wrote. It is also a change of scene—a squishy, stinky and grotesquely noisy scene, but sometimes I'll take that. It's something to do that isn't another afternoon in the bloody living room.

Nevertheless, you must be mentally prepared for the experience. Shit is about to get real. Psych yourself up like you are going into battle. Here's what you can expect from your soft-play adventure . . .

- Upon entering the building, your senses will be overloaded. The sights, the sounds, the smells. Kids will be charging around like monkeys on speed. You will initially feel like you are drowning in a sea of screaming Hello Kitty tights and snotty noses, but after half an hour your eyes and ears will become quite accustomed to this annoying orchestra.

- The whining and screams of "joy" merge into a steady background hum, interjected only with panicked shouts of "Do you need a wee?" and your own *If you can't play nicely, we'll go home!* (This threat is never executed because you have still not asked your friend about that text from the fit bloke at work, or drunk your now-tepid coffee, so, despite your children having no interest in each other, they will enjoy this playdate if it kills you.)

- Your socks will be wet. Mostly, this will be from Robinsons Fruit Shoot spillage, but you should know that at other times your socks will be soggy because you have stepped in piss. Or vomit. I was first on the scene at a Category One Soft-Play Emergency once, when a newly "potty-trained" toddler shat on the slide. This could happen. Be strong.

- Trips to soft-play centers will remind you why you largely dislike other people's children (and, at times, if we're being honest, your own). They charge around like savages, and nothing is more infuriating than the "bigger" boys and girls who insist on hurtling through the *baby* area. *It says "Under 5s," you prick.*

- Understand that the owners of soft-play-hell labyrinths need to make money. It is a business, not a safe haven for mums who've lost the will to live in their living rooms. You will therefore be encouraged to buy overpriced soggy paninis and jugs of lemonade. And boiling-hot tea, which you will try not to spill on the feral children running between the Play Zone and Tumble Tot areas.

- "Children must be supervised at all times" state the Rules of Play. *Ha ha ha ha.* This does not happen. There are parents at large who have misinterpreted "supervision" to mean letting *another* child's parent manage the situation while they sit on plastic chairs generally not giving a toss. It is not your job to keep lifting little Sammy over the squashy steps or to tell bigger boy Billy to stop elbowing everyone in the head. Do these people think you come here in the hope of taking charge of their unruly kids? That you enjoy being the fucking Pied Piper of soft-play strays? You must glare at the child and ask loudly, "Where are your parents?" *Everyone* has to suffer. That is the real Rule of Play. Having said that, one of my favorite ever comments on my blog was a mum of two slightly older children noting that she had done her fair share of soft-play running around (after everybody's children) when hers were little so had earned the right to kick back with a hot chocolate and *Heat*. "I've served my time," she wrote. This gives me hope for the future.

- One word of warning is to watch what you wear. *Don't* wear low-rise jeans. At some point, your rescue services will be required at the top of the squashy play warren and you will end up scaling five yards of rope netting to collect your child with the top half of your knickers on show. I was still wearing rather fetching (and large) M&S cotton maternity pants for the best part of a year postbirth. Nobody needs to see that when they're enjoying a soggy panini. The same goes for low-cut tops. I misplaced a breast pad in the ball pool once—I probably forgot to reclasp the old feeding bra, or maybe I just neglected to tuck my boob back in at all. I wonder if it's still there somewhere . . . I dread to think what else is submerged beneath those balls: other lost breast pads, hair bands, plasters . . . We should just accept that the most appropriate attire for such outings is leggings and a T-shirt. Or high-waisted jeans. And remember to pack socks . . . because the aforementioned sock sogginess is still preferable to the risk of a verruca.

- You will "catch up" with your friend in ten-second chunks of conversation only, these chunks sandwiched between your combined offsprings' food/loo/behavioral issues. "I'm thinking of applying for a new job, actually, but—*Will you stop climbing up the slide?*—Did I tell you what happened at Claire's sweep? She was already three centimeters dilated and—*Come here*, now, *Mummy's getting* really cross!" Eventually, once you've got the gist of each other's life updates, it's time to make a move.

- It then goes without saying that your children won't want to leave this noisy hellhole. There may be tears and/or protest planking in the Mega Maze. That's why you must *always* make sure you have backup unhealthy-snack bribes to entice them back to the car. And wine in the fridge when you get back home, obviously.

I should note that if you go in half term, or with a gin hangover from the previously mentioned night out, soft play is much worse than an afternoon in the living room. It's total carnage. Just stick *Megamind* on.

"I *hate* soft play. There's no collaborative play or negotiation going on. It's just sugar-fueled children intent on inflicting maximum pain on each other via the mediums of plastic-ball throwing, trampoline ninja-kicking or three-pronged attacks down the slide onto unsuspecting toddlers. It's the infant equivalent to *Lord of the Flies.*"
JOANNE, SUNDERLAND

What a Mess
(I Blame the Toys)

I HAVE LOST COUNT of the number of times James and I have found ourselves staring, with slightly pained expressions, at the chaos that is our living space. Home is where the heart is, by all accounts, but I can't say my heart belongs to the house I'm living in at the moment, despite having been there for three years. We eat and sleep in it, I spend at least four days a week begging my children to calm down and stop charging around inside it, but it's a far cry from the family *home* we'd had in mind.

Perhaps it was foolish of us to buy a "project"—though, in our defense, it was the one and only house we could afford at the time so we put an offer in despite the laminate flooring smelling of wet dog. It ticked enough boxes (three bedrooms, not in the ghetto) and although it was far from ideal (no bath, no utility room, no useful storage of any kind, no parking, horrendous and worryingly phallic 1970s mushroom-patterned tiles), we were like Kirstie and Phil's dream-property hunters— we saw the *potential*.

Unfortunately, property potential amounts to jack shit when you have neither the funds nor the time to realize that potential. There is no spare DIY time when you own small people. We had not thought it through and now live in a constant state of "We'll sort it out at the weekend/next month/next summer." Three years' worth of failed weekend/next month/next summer sort-out promises have left us with some interesting quirks. There are times when I couldn't care less about our habitable (but ultimately a bit shit) house. But, sometimes, the frustration of not easily being able to fix things with the kids around annoys me beyond belief. And, I've discovered, James is the same (hence our pained expressions and lots of sighing).

Pre-kids, we simply would not have put up with a barely usable sink and a hallway chandelier light with no bulbs (we were supposed to investigate both the leaky washbasin and nonstandard bulb sizes back when we moved in). Never in a month of Sundays would we have made do with an old bed-sheet as a curtain because the blind fell down (we were supposed to investigate stronger blind-fitting options . . . about two years ago). Pre-kids, if somebody had suggested that I would start—but fail to complete—painting the hideous mahogany kitchen units, I would have laughed in their face. (Nobody is that bloody lazy; clearly, you wouldn't make do with a half-painted kitchen, for God's sake . . . oh, right, yep, that's now on next summer's To Sort Out list, too.) Given that the pair of us struggle to find the time to fart without the boys interrupting, I think it's a fair assumption that this ever-multiplying list will be rolled over forevermore (at least until we come to sell the house and an estate agent tells us the penis tiles really have to go).

And then there's the general mess. Home may not be where the heart is, but it's certainly where all the crap is. And, as we engage in regular look-at-the-sodding-state-of-the-place conversations, we've discovered we share a common hatred toward the things we regard as the root cause of this endless untidiness: *toys*.

Unless you have the luxury of a playroom (future goal right there), a previously uncluttered living space becomes the Early Learning Center with a raisin infestation. You can try to tidy up throughout the day (by putting stuff back into various Swedish toy-storage solutions), but you will soon realize you're pissing against the wind. A small piece of my soul dies every time I hear the crash of Lego bricks hitting the carpet. Despite attempts to scoop them all up, I know that when I later go to check on Henry sleeping I'll end up with a stray brick impaled on the underside of my foot. ("Good night, my angel. Sleep tight, love you—*Oww! Bastard Lego!*") I'm always finding toys in unexpected places, too: Power Rangers in the shower, Mr. Potato Head's ear in my handbag—I once found myself in bed with a Buzz, and I'm not talking the Ann Summers variety.

That's not my only beef with toys. In fact, I've written an

entire list dedicated to the reasons I hate toys, possibly prompted by the most recent Lego foot-impaling incident . . .

My Beef with Toys

- You cannot get rid of them. The moment you start boxing up unloved toys for charity/eBay/the baby next door is the moment the previously neglected item becomes the *best toy ever*. That plastic tractor from the bottom of the basket he has never played with? Best toy ever, one of his favorites. Half a Sofia the First tea set gathering dust on the bookcase? Best toy ever, one of his favorites. (I have resorted to silently swiping toys in the dead of night and shelving them ready for removal, but Henry knows. I think he does a toy stocktake every morning.) A friend of mine had me wetting myself laughing when she described the time she had cleared out "a load of crap" for a school jumble sale only for her son to have the mother of all meltdowns about being parted from the toys he'd never played with. She ended up paying money to buy back all her own crap. Kids are weird.

- They come with *ridiculous* amounts of packaging. Once you've got through the cardboard, the plastic and the sodding metal ties, you will sometimes need a screwdriver to free your child's Christmas toy from its box. I ended up out of breath and sweating after battling to free Optimus Prime. What the chuff is that about? I thought we were trying to cut down on waste these days.

- There are *never* enough batteries. Unless you are an Organized Mum and have them stowed away in a cupboard alongside candles and blank greeting cards (I have no such cupboard, so birthdays are always fun in our house), you will be forever running out of batteries. We sacrifice batteries from the DVD remote to keep Fireman Sam's Ocean Rescue Center in operation ("No film tonight, love, but at least Pontypandy is safe"). And when toys do have working batteries, they are quite—often unbearably—annoying. I had to take the batteries *out* of Alfie Bear (if you don't have an Alfie Bear, this is not a void I suggest you fill). It's not Alfie's fault, but after five hours of "I'm a friendly light-up bear, I'll teach you one, two, three," I have been known to hunt down that screwdriver for battery extraction and mutter, "Not so friendly now, are you, Alfie?" He is currently mute, discarded in a toy basket (but is still the best toy ever, one of Henry's favorites, if ever this was in doubt).

- They break and everyone cries. The freebie toys from magazines and plastic tat from discount stores where things cost around £1 are the usual suspects, leading to tears of disappointment and the dishonest "We'll fix it later!" promise. I have a "fix it later" drawer full of sad toys waiting in vain for somebody to buy some superglue. This will never happen—we will throw them out following the aforementioned look-at-the-sodding-state-of-the-place conversation.

- Toys with hundreds of random pieces can piss off. I swear I own rogue pieces that never belonged to an original puzzle or game and have simply appeared like a toy plague—but I daren't chuck them out (because of the stocktake). By the same token, there are the toys that go missing. Hats off to anyone who's managed to keep the phone attached to the baby walker, and where the hell do those squeaky eggs go? Small toy pieces also become a genuine safety concern when you have an orally investigative baby on a mission to stick bricks down his windpipe. I spend my life shouting, "Don't leave it on the floor—your brother could choke!"

- They are an eyesore. Even if we were to get our arses in gear and sort out the house, we'd still face this issue. There is simply nothing trendy about a multicolored jigsaw foam mat. *Ideal Home* never features a strategically placed Playmobil recycling truck or a statement Jumperoo, does it? You might as well forget whatever home-interior theme it was that you originally had in mind—unless you were aiming for "Plastic-Tat Chic."

- The price of them is extortionate. Aside from the discount-stores-where-things-cost-around-£1 items (purchased in an attempt to placate the whining between Next and Boots), toys are preposterously expensive. I begrudge paying a small fortune for toys that are often quite basic. Once you've invested, there is also the danger that your child will lose interest in the TV program you, arguably, should have bloody shares in, given the merchandise you own.

"I don't like *Fireman Sam* anymore; it's for babies."

Say what? You've got to be shitting me. Time to start making noises about having a clear-out—he'll soon reclaim them as his *best toys ever*...

I'd like to take this opportunity to say how terribly sorry I am to all my friends who became parents before I did. In particular, I'm sorry for buying your children modeling clay, craft sets and toys with gazillions of pieces. I thought these were fun activities you would get out on a rainy Sunday afternoon before returning them to their rightful boxes. *I didn't know.* Forgive me. xx

"Polly Pocket. No words can describe the pain of standing on that little cow in the middle of the night."
LAUREN, CORNWALL

Things I Swore I Wouldn't Do as a Parent (but Do)

"Don't you just hate it when parents do that?" I used to ask James with a chuckle, discussing all manner of annoying parental habits, safe in the knowledge that whatever "that" was, you would never find me doing it. I didn't have kids back then, obviously. The joke is now on me.

I lift up my infant to smell his bum

Not a quick sniff of the general area but a deep, investigative inhalation of nappy aroma achieved by burying my face deep into the arse of his sleepsuit. Prechildren, I once heard a mum comment, "You know it's not your own baby's poo when it's a *foreign smell*." I had a little chuckle to myself about how sad her life must be.

Three years later, and I'm pretty confident I could pick Jude's nappy out of a twenty-strong nappy-sniff test. They should add that as a round to *The Cube*.

I refer to my husband as "Daddy"

(And no, this isn't in any way kinky.) I have tried *so* hard not to do this, not to become one of those couples who are happy to exist purely as Mummy and Daddy. But now and again I let myself down and ask James, "Do you want a cup of tea, Daddy?" before looking around and realizing the kids are in bed. And Daddy hasn't even batted an eyelid at the loss of his actual name. *Arghhhh*.

I care less about what I look like

Not all the time—there are times when I care more. (I care quite a lot when I know I'm going to come into contact with people who knew me before I incubated two small humans, my worst nightmare being them thinking that I have "let myself go.") But daily life with kids gets in the way of self-maintenance, and sometimes I neglect to shave my legs, lazily throw my hoodie on again (the comfy one with the baked-beans stain) and find myself standing in the kitchen shoveling fish fingers into my gob straight from the baking tray. In those moments I conclude that, yes, I have indeed let myself go.

I tell lies

Sometimes, a lie is the only way to conclude things. "Oh no, look, the bakery is shut, sweetheart, so we can't have any cakes today!" spoken as I hastily steer one or the other of my children past the open bakery because I have no parenting backbone and cannot be arsed to put my foot down with a no.

I have, at least, discovered I'm not alone in occasionally offering a slightly stretched version of the truth for the sake of ending an otherwise infinite conversation. A friend of mine recently posted on Facebook the following transcript of a conversation she had with her three-year-old, under the heading "I'm way too tired for this . . .":

Chester:	When Daddy was a little boy, did he live with Granny and Grandad?
Me:	Yes.
Chester:	Where was I?
Me:	You weren't anywhere, as you weren't born yet.
Chester:	Was I big?
Me:	No.
Chester:	Was I little?
Me:	No.
Chester:	Was I in the jungle?
Me:	Yes. Yes, you were.

I comment, "Gosh, she's grown!" every time I see the offspring of friends or family

I mean, it's kind of a given, isn't it? Kids grow. Daily. If you don't see your goddaughter for six months, it is highly probable she will have got bigger. Regardless, I always feel the urge to say, "She's getting so big now!" and/or, "Look how grown-up they both are!" as a conversation starter at any social gathering. I'm really boring.

I talk crap (actual crap)

Engaging in detailed dialogue about things which are neither interesting nor particularly savory has become a talent of mine. A firm favorite is a comprehensive chat with James about the size/color/consistency of our offspring's excrement:

"That was a nasty one—look, it's got, like, tiny black wormy things in it!"
"I think that's the banana coming out. It was like that last night, so I
    googled it."
"I much prefer it when they're a bit more solid."
"Me, too."
"Fucking hell, we're sad."

Perhaps we've resorted to this humdrum debriefing about nappy contents and other dull matters (when Jude had his nap/how much of his sandwich Henry ate at lunchtime/it having been "good drying weather") because we've discovered that attempting any kind of grown-up conversation with small people at large is pointless.

Occasionally, we forget this lesson and start talking seriously about our work meetings/mortgage rates/weekend plans, but after being interrupted every third word and dodging toys that are being thrown at our heads, we forget what we were going to say anyway.

I bribe my children

"I'll never bribe my children," I once said. *Ha ha ha ha*. Bribery is actually the sole parenting "tactic" I've mastered that seems to produce favorable results. I'm not alone in this: bribery is the backbone of parenting for 99 percent of the population.* Behind every well-behaved child there are Percy Pigs, right? The remaining 1 percent are using some kind of witchcraft or sorcery.

Maybe we ought to stop being so hard on ourselves and just modify what we call this tactic; rather than *bribing* our children, we're simply making use of coercion, negotiation and rewards. We're teaching our children that their actions and behavior have consequences, as in:

"If you eat all your salad, you can have a biscuit."

"If you behave nicely at Hey Let's Play, you can have a biscuit."

"If you let Mummy phone the insurance company in peace for a moment, she'll give you a biscuit."

Balls, there's definitely a biscuit theme here. I'm genuinely having a pang of worry about the boys' teeth now, so in future, I'm going to ~~ration the biscuits~~ brush them for longer.

I shout

At home. In the car. In Primark. I know it all looks a bit *Shameless* and it doesn't ever solve the problem, but, on a bad day, that's just how I roll. It's bloody difficult not to lose

---

*Based on no scientific study or opinion-poll survey; in fact, this is a completely unsubstantiated figure.

your temper as a parent. (See "Just One of Those Days," page 205.)

I also nag . . .

Like a broken record of parental fussiness, repeating instructions that nobody (least of all my children) is listening to, like, "Can everybody just calm down a bit?" "Play *nicely!*" and "We're not going anywhere until you stop whining!" The latter will be said as we exit the house, while everybody is very much still whining because escape to anywhere is better than confinement in the house.

. . . and make ridiculous empty threats

Alongside the general warnings issued to get arses out of the door, I often hear myself threatening disproportionate consequences that are both unenforceable and unwise:

"Right, I'm not going to tell you again: no more TV for the week!" (As soon as this comes out of my mouth, I realize it's an error—how the hell would I make lunch, for a start?)

"I'm phoning Father Christmas in a minute to get your name taken off the list. There will be no chance to make amends this time." (Shitballs, what a stupid thing to say, and it's only August.)

"Say good-bye to all of your favorite toys; they are going to the dump." (Henry has cottoned on to the fact that his mummy is a bit highly strung and simply waits for me to calm down before quietly retrieving the toys from the "take to the dump" pile in our bedroom.)

I use baby talk

I give every object a nickname. Milk becomes "milkies."
Bottle becomes "bot bots." Nappies become "nap naps." Soft
toys become "snuggies" or "bunnykins." Just the other day I
said to my husband (and I quote), "If you sort out his bot
bots, I'll change his nap naps and find his snuggies." *What
a twat.* This use of language is bloody annoying for all concerned, but it's what parents do.

That said, there is something quite comforting about not
caring and just enjoying those babyish moments. When I
go in to get Jude first thing in the morning I pick him up
and say, without any embarrassment, "Good morning, my
Angel Plum Plums." I don't know why or how he became
my Angel Plum Plums, but that is what he is. And a bloody
lovely Angel Plum Plums he is, too. If this were a Facebook
status I'd be inserting a heart emoji here, alongside an angel and a plum.

"I definitely did not catch myself at work saying,
'Uh-Oh-Printer' as I loaded another toner
cartridge. Definitely not."
OWEN, POOLE

Why It's Fine to Reminisce About Before

CHATTING TO JAMES about what life was like before we became parents is one of my all-time favorite pastimes. The conversation usually goes something like this:

"Do you remember when I used to say, 'Shall we go for a walk, or some fresh air?' and we would just go out for a walk or some fresh air? Right then! Without packing a bag! Unbelievable!"

"Do you remember when we had chats about how our days at work had been over dinner? Do you remember when we had proper chats? Do you remember when we had proper dinner?"

"Do you remember when we went to the Dominican Republic and, aside from a token monster-truck excursion to a sugar plantation, we did nothing but swim and sunbathe for three weeks? *Three weeks!* We even had sex in the afternoon!"

Though I have met lots of parents who share my "God, I'd kill for a duvet day!" sentiment, I sometimes question whether I am looking back at our pre-parent existence a little too much—particularly when I meet parents who don't seem to wistfully reflect on life before their children arrived at *all*.

Pre-parent Nostalgia Spectrum

0 = "I cannot remember life before we were blessed with children, nor would I want to."

5 = "I do miss the odd lie-in."

10 = "I just want to eat my food in peace and not have to do a speed poo with both children hanging off my ankles and not have bladder/sneezing issues and not have to buy the budget supermarket shampoo. Do you remember when we had disposable income? Do you remember when I had actual boobs, not *small, empty sacks*?!"

Yes, I am a 10.

But every now and then, I deliberately stop myself harking back to the good old days, because an increasingly familiar feeling of guilt creeps in (see "Mum Guilt," page 217) and leads me to reason as follows:

Persistently thinking back to life before becoming a mum

must signify regret for having joined the Motherhood and a lack of appreciation for having had children.

I persistently think back to life before becoming a mum.

Therefore, I do not appreciate my children.

This is, of course, just daft. I *do* appreciate my children and—shaky, guilt-ridden days aside (when everything you do/don't do makes you feel like a terrible parent)—I see no reason why we should feel bad about this reminiscing. In fact, I would go so far as to say we should *celebrate* the *before* days for all they represent:

Spontaneity

Uninterrupted sleep

Going to the cinema to watch something without Minions in it

Having something to get dressed up for (outside of Wednesday's Stay and Play)

Having time to browse

Having money to *buy*

Those wild nights out which ended in dirty kebabs and blister plasters

"Popping" anywhere in under an hour

Having a tantrum-free dinner

Having an efficient pelvic floor

Sunbathing with your eyes shut

Reading in peace (doing *anything* in peace)

Devouring a grown-up ice cream like a Magnum in its entirety and not having to donate it to the toddler who has dropped the bottom third of his Rocket...

When my (then) two-year-old lay on the floor at the bottom of the escalator in a shopping center, screaming, *"Help me, I'm stuck! Fire! Call Fireman Sam!"* (he wasn't stuck; there was no fire), I remembered with great fondness the days when I could actually *look* at clothes while out shopping. And try them on. Without getting red and sweaty. Without taking somebody's ankles out with the stroller. Without swearing.

When I had a nasty chest infection last year (and felt pretty bloody sorry for myself), I couldn't help but think back to poorly days spent in bed with a Lemsip. I also couldn't help but curse the fact that I was already downstairs at seven a.m. watching *Mickey Mouse Clubhouse*, mustering up the strength to wrestle the baby into a new nappy and wondering why Mickey is such a prick. ("Hot dog, hot dog, hot diggety dog . . ." *Kill . . . me . . .*)

Every time a heat wave is promised, I can't help but crave the days of basking in the sun without being consumed by infant-sunburn worries. Days when I didn't spend the day running around slathering everyone in SPF 50 and constantly repositioning the baby's sun hat. (We weren't prepared for our second-born to come out quite so . . . quite so . . . *ginger*. He could easily pass as Damian Lewis's love child. This has only heightened the need to keep the sun hat on him.)

Do I miss life before motherhood?

Yes, sometimes I miss life before motherhood.

Sometimes, when the end of my tether has been well and truly reached and I'm *so bloody done in*, I long for that old life back. To relive it.

But I don't *genuinely* wish to go back there, because the

situation is different now. It's true that my life is no longer carefree or spontaneous. It's true I really would like to enjoy a mealtime without somebody crying. It's true I quite liked it when my pelvic floor was intact. But, between the tiredness and the cursing at oversize rodents singing about hot dogs, I can hand on heart say I wouldn't change it (unless I had a license to borrow Marty McFly's time machine and head back to 2008 once a month on a Sunday, in which case I totally would).

I spend significantly more time celebrating my life *as* a parent than I do reflecting on the glory of life when I was not. Every day provides a celebration of the *after* days, because spending time with my boys knocks spots off all the other stuff from days gone by. So I hope I am in no way being unfaithful to the special life I now have with my boys by remembering what my life was like before them.

I am simply remembering a different time, which was a special time in its own right.

These days, when other parents declare, "God, I can't even remember what life was like without the kids, can you?" I mostly stick to up-front honesty.

"Yes, I bloody can. It was beautiful."

Part Three

THE SECOND TIME AROUND

"The risk of a dirty protest in
the waiting room was a genuine one."

Having Another One

I RECKON WE MANAGED approximately six months of parenthood before the subtle SCI (Second-Child Interrogation) started. "When's Henry going to have a little brother or sister?" they asked ("they" as in the world, his wife and their nosy sodding dog). Had we thought about the ideal age gap? Had we planned when we would start trying? Wasn't it lucky we already had the three-bedroom house to accommodate the second baby?! Cue rabbit-in-the-headlights face.

What was the right thing to say and do here? I racked my brain for a politer way of saying, "You must be fucking joking!" because, quite honestly, at that stage, i.e., during Henry's first year and, in fact, some months beyond it, the idea of bringing another sleep-stealing bairn into the world was not one I was prepared to entertain. The first year of motherhood had not *exactly* lived up to my expectations, though, in hindsight, those expectations were probably derived from a Boots *Parenting Club* article where a mum with very white teeth threw her nonrefluxy baby in the air on a warm spring day.

At Henry's first birthday party, I can quite vividly remember thinking, "I love him at this age and I'm enjoying this bit." I felt as though I had settled into my role as mum. But that same day I can also remember looking over at somebody else's newborn baby and thinking, "Sod that for a game of soldiers." I was just starting to feel like myself again, with Henry sleeping through the night, and chatting to me (sort of) and making me laugh. I did feel slightly guilty for having wished his first year away, but I was still quietly glad the baby bit was done and dusted. The worst was over.

So I found the constant SCI questions really exasperating. I knew that the people who were asking them were well meaning and just expressing their curiosity about the shape our family would take. But at times I felt quite troubled by the fact that it was simply *assumed* we would be having another one. As if it must just be a question of *when* because we'd be foolish to have "just the one."

"Loads of people have one child and live happily ever after. I actually can't see us having any more," I eventually began to tell people. I hoped that would halt the questioning.

"But you can't have just one!" came the replies. "Wouldn't it be a shame for poor Henry?" "You'll regret it." "Don't leave it too late!"

We continued to present our united "one and done" stance and, mostly, people stopped asking. But I still felt an unspoken pressure to give it more thought, not least because Thou Shalt Have Two Children is like an unwritten commandment in our family: you have two children (with a gap of somewhere between two and four years) because, well, because *that is just what you do*. I'm one of two siblings; James is one of two siblings; our respective siblings each have two children. It's as if they all employed the Goldilocks and the Three Bears logic of child numbers:

One is not enough (and is lonely).

Three is too many (and a bit crazy; you'd need a new car, for a start).

Two is *just right*.

So, despite telling anybody who would listen that we had no plans for a second ("God, no, zero desire to activate the self-destruct button here, ta!"), I'm sure the general consensus, particularly among our family, was simply that we would come round to the idea. "You'll change your mind!" they said . . .

And I guess *they*, the two-child enforcers, were right because our story doesn't end with Henry as our only child. We must have "come round to the idea," right? Something must have happened to make us broody and tempt us to get back on the babycoaster?

Well, kind of.

Jude was, after all, another planned pregnancy. I've pledged total honesty in this book, and I would tell you if he was a "surprise" (or, indeed, an Oopsie Baby, as I once read on a parenting forum; I do hope baby Oopsie doesn't grow up with a complex). But no, just like his big brother, the bun was intentionally sited in the oven.

So what changed?

It certainly *wasn't* my overall maternal broodiness. I waited in vain to start longing for another baby and no broody feelings surfaced.

But I just had this niggle.

And when I told James about my niggle it turned out he had it, too. It wasn't tied to a feeling of duty to "avoid" an only child, as we had already decided quite confidently that having happy parents was more instrumental to our child's well-being than having parents unhappily engineer him a sibling. But *something* was niggling. When people talked to me about having more children and I said, "We're happy with one, thanks!" I no longer felt like I said it with such conviction. I was starting to doubt myself. And, as we approached Henry's second Christmas, we began to engage in the Chat all over again. We faced the niggle head-on and, after a good few hours of conversation, we concluded that yes, we would try for another baby. What follows is a summation of our reasoning:

We always thought we would have two children. When we discussed our vision of "life in ten years' time" there were *always* two children in the picture. Two children in the back of the car, two children with us on holiday, two children at the dinner table . . . a happy family of four.

It was true that, as the owners of an almost-two-year-old, we were quite happy with our lot. It was also true we had no desire to have another *baby*. Zero desire to be pregnant or battle through those early months again. But looking ahead at the long term, taking the immediate reality of babies and toddlers out of the equation, we were still picturing ourselves with two.

Our vision was still intact and had manifested itself as a niggle. I suppose it's just possible we'd internalized the aspirational norm of being a 2.4-child family, but I suspected it wasn't that at all. It wasn't just about somebody to keep Henry company; it was about completing our family. (And, on a selfish level, we did discuss how we hoped it would "pay off" because as older siblings, they would entertain each other and we would be able to sunbathe and drink mojitos on holiday.)

Whether we liked it or not, our second child, the one from Our Vision, was simply not going to appear by process of teleportation into the back of our car or at the dinner table. We knew all too well the real process required to get to that point.

So, no, we didn't really change our minds about wanting another *baby* but focused instead on our agreement that we *did* want another child. It was decided at the beginning of December 2013 that we would "go for it," and there was no time to rethink our decision, because I was pregnant by New Year's Eve.

Had I focused on the whole baby bit, I'm not sure I would ever have done it again. This seems mad now, as Jude turned out to be a delightful baby and a total legend. (If you're reading this, Henry, my darling, please know you were a lovely baby and a legend, too, in your own special vomiting and nap-refusing way . . . you just really blossomed at age one.)

I recently found myself, for the first time ever, looking at a newborn baby and thinking, "Ahhh, I really miss that snuggly baby stage." I may even have momentarily thought, "Maybe we could just have one more," as I sniffed said baby's head with fondness.

I'm now slightly fearful that, as I approach thirty, a genuine hormonal broodiness is creeping up on me for the first time, as if Mother Nature is telling me, "Now's your time."

Perhaps *now* is the time I should have started having children. Perhaps I was four or five years too early to the baby party.

It would certainly explain a lot.

"On our return from our mini-break weekend the toddler got travel sick. The only thing to hand was his welly . . . and then the eight-month-old did a smelly poo. So I found myself sat between two car seats holding a welly full of sick while breathing in shitty vapors. It was a great drive home."

JULIE, DEVON

One to Two: What's the Deal?

As well as the interrogation about "having another one," it also used to quietly piss me off that, when I mentioned how hard I was finding looking after Henry, how I was struggling after a bad night or a meltdown on the bus, the stock response was always "Just you wait until you have two!" (Because I couldn't possibly be struggling with "just the one," obviously.) I *was* struggling.

I overheard another mum saying something at a playgroup once which has turned out to be a pretty fair assessment. She was talking in a group of "one-child" mums about the arrival of her second child, and she reflected, "I'm worrying less with her [her second baby] because I have less time to worry, and I've realized that much of what I found impossible with him [her first baby] was stuff I was making impossible for myself.

It *was* easier with one, but I couldn't have known that then. The benefit of hindsight, eh?"

There was definitely something in that. Every so often, James and I reflect fondly on our lives with one child in much the same way that we reflected on our lives with no children and find ourselves saying things like, "God, wasn't it easy with one! Why didn't we take Henry abroad? It would have been *so easy* with one." But, mostly, we stop ourselves, because the fact of the matter is we would not have found it easy. We found everything hard, partly because we overobsessed about how we were doing things and partly because whether you have one child or ten children, it can still be bloody tough going.

I may jokingly have posted a Facebook status which read: "What's it like having two?" "Well, like having one, but worse."

Actually, I haven't found having two *that* much harder than having one, though I'm sure it's different for everyone. For me, possibly the biggest adjustment about becoming a parent in the first place was accepting that my life was no longer my own. It was no longer my own from the moment we drove newborn Henry home from the hospital via the McDonald's drive-thru (yes, that was his first-ever outing). To be honest, my life is not really any *less* my own with two children and there is certainly no doubt I've mentally found the jump from one child to two children easier than the First-Child Hurricane (not least because Jude has been slightly less of a crier and more of a napper).

But—and it's not an insignificant but—there are certain logistical challenges to having two small children we just never considered when we had one, and there are a couple of instances which really stick in my mind as times when I truly felt the strain of an extra child. So here's the lowdown on the trickiest bits.

You Only Have One Pair of Hands

I know this sounds pretty obvious, but there have been many times since making the jump from one to two when I have genuinely not known which child to tend to. And which one to neglect.

The worst such occasion to date was the first time I had the misfortune of taking both the boys to see the doctor. As we sat in the waiting room, with ten minutes to spare before Jude's eight-week check, I thought I was doing quite well. We were on time, and nobody was crying. Things started to get a little tense when Henry got off his seat and lay facedown on the floor of the waiting room. When I asked him what he was doing, he shouted, *"I'm resting!"* and, as I was midbreastfeed, I didn't quite know what to do. He wasn't screaming and nobody had complained about having to step over him on their way to reception, so I figured it would cause less fuss if I just left him there.

And then, at the *exact* moment Jude started kicking off (windy or tired, one of the two), the newly potty-trained Henry announced that he needed the loo. There is only one loo at the surgery we go to, and it is not big enough to fit the pram in.

I hadn't planned for this dilemma.

After it became apparent Henry couldn't hold it (he was doing the Wee Dance), I had no choice but to pass the baby to a very kind but completely randomly chosen old lady so I could fulfill loo duty. I am relatively certain I would not have left a total stranger in charge of my baby the first time around (understandably, it is not the Done Thing). But on this occasion my gut told me that getting to the loo was the priority and, judging by Henry's worsening waddle, the risk of a dirty protest in the waiting room was a genuine one.

It was a good job we didn't chance it, as it soon became apparent he had indeed chosen this particular moment for his daily poo. Marvelous. I'd never before felt quite as torn as I did that day: knowing I needed to hold Henry on the loo to finish his poo but equally feeling immensely anxious that my poor abandoned baby might just have become the plot inspiration for the next season of *The Missing*.

Mission Poo finally accomplished, I was relieved to find that the kind old lady hadn't snatched my baby. She was, in fact, holding him up in the air, and he was laughing his head off, obviously delighted with his new Granny Stranger.

Granny Stranger then informed me that during the time we'd spent in the loo, we had missed the call for our appointment and somebody else had gone in instead. So the now very tired Jude had to wait another twenty minutes for the doctor while Henry proudly counseled the other patients on loo hygiene: "You must wash your hands! Bottom, bottom, farty pants!"

I immediately texted James to inform him that I would never, ever be taking *his* two children to the doctor again.

Sometimes, the Stress Is Doubled

When you have two (or *more*—Jesus, I can't even imagine!), embarking on a proper outing (getting in the car/catching the bus/packing up a day bag, etc.) can be more than a bit stressful.

I was alerted to the reality of this new dynamic one day when I woke up full of parenting courage and decided I would take both of my children (one just turned three years, the other five months old, at the time) to the beach.

In the car.

On my own.

The day before, I had found myself pissed off beyond words at being stuck in the house with a crying baby and his brother running from one end of the lounge to the other (and back again), shouting, "You'll never catch me!" so on this day I decided on a whim that we were going out.

"Right, boys, we're going to the beach!" I declared. Unplanned and unpacked, this felt quite . . . *liberating*. Henry got quite excited, and I decided this must be what Fun Mum feels like.

"Let's go to the beach! Right now!" God, I can be so much fun!

This was at nine a.m. We would pack a bag and leave immediately, I told them.

It was 11:47 when we got in the car.

From the birth of my plan to the moment we were all strapped in the car, *three hours* had passed. I won't bore you with the full breakdown of those hours because if you are a parent, you will simply *know* how bloody impossible it is to get out of the house (and if you're not yet a parent, trust me, there *are* days when it is bloody impossible to get out of the house). But on this day in particular, the added bonus of an extra child to get sorted just made it seem harder. There were several nappies, two bottles, at least ten ounces of vomit (always a pleasure, Jude) and one fairly major "I'm not putting any clothes on" tantrum from Henry, which morphed into a tantrum about "Cat," the sun shade, as soon as we got in the car (Cat had fallen down and he couldn't pet it). Life is unbearably unfair when you've just turned three and everything is conspiring against you, including cat-shaped sun shades.

Henry then proceeded to shout, at regular two-minute intervals, over the *top* of his brother's crying, "Why are we going this way?" "Are we lost?" "Put the *sally nav* on!" (It's lucky he didn't remember the previous road trip, when I ended up yelling, "There isn't anywhere to turn around, you stupid bitch!" at poor "Sally Nav.")

When we finally arrived at the seafront, I couldn't find a parking space; I'd forgotten it was sodding *half term*. There isn't much regard for half terms and summer holidays when you are on maternity leave and every day is one almighty Groundhog. I finally found a space to squeeze into and nervously eyed the large groups of people.

I'd packed sandwiches and had imagined an idyllic tartanblanket picnic on the beach, but, as Jude had just got to sleep (and I was drinking in the lack of crying), we ate it in the car. I felt proper sorry for Henry because, had it just been the two of us, we would have eaten our sarnies on the beach. Instead, we admired the sea view from the Astra.

When Jude woke up, we headed out. I had a plan. We would go for a walk along the seafront first (with the pram), and then we would shove everything back into the car and take just our merry selves onto the beach. "I could totally handle this two-child parenting on my own," I thought.

I was stressed within two minutes.

Though Henry had previously been adamant that he didn't need a wee, the old "I'm desperate" jig surfaced again and we had to *run* to the loos. When we got there, despite my nagging warnings, he touched pretty much every visible inch of drug-taker-wee-infested loo rim. I, too, needed a wee, which I performed by hovering with the cubicle door wedged open by the pram. We then washed our hands in a sink which looked equally as contaminated as the loo, and I was left wondering if I should order a DIY disease-test kit.

Jude started crying because he was hungry.

Henry ran back along the seafront, fell over, hurt his hands and joined in with the crying.

When we finally made it to the beach for our fun family outing, I sat on the sand feeding Jude while Henry proceeded to give me a heart attack by shouting, "I'm burying a dog poo!" which, he later clarified, was "just pretend." (Something is wrong with a child whose buried treasure is pretend dog shit, no?)

We walked down to the sea, with me holding Jude and Henry holding my hand. That was nice. I mean, that was actually really *nice*. I breathed in air that didn't exist in my living room and had a moment. I patted myself on the back for braving the adventure. I may even have Instagrammed it (#beach lifewithmybestones).

And then, after a final poo from Jude, whose nappy I awkwardly changed in the boot of the car, it was time to go home. Naturally, Henry didn't want to go home, so I got down on his level and reasoned with him about why we were leaving. (I bribed him with a Creme Egg.)

ON BOTH the aforementioned occasions, and others besides, the dynamic of having two has indeed proved a bit more testing.

But we were feeling pretty tested already.

Girl or Boy? (What You're Not Allowed to Wish For)

SINCE BECOMING a parent I have had a fair few thoughts and said a fair few things I have later gone on to feel guilty about. Things I now find it hard to admit to. Usually, these have not been true feelings at all but spur-of-the-moment outbursts brought on by the frustration of another bleedin' night feed or a protest-planking toddler. We all say things we don't mean in the heat of the moment, and I have said many things I don't really mean about my boys. Never directly *to* them (unless you count the sweary rants at them when they were babies, when I'm pretty sure they were none the wiser); they are usually directed at James; or at nobody in particular, as I stare at the ceiling grinding my teeth. They are flashes of resentment that are less regret about having children and more regret about finding myself sitting, covered in baby sick, completely off my face with tiredness, psyching myself up to "offer the second breast."

One time, after a particularly hairy night with Jude (who was a couple of months old), I woke at around five a.m. to find Henry in our bed with soaking-wet pajamas. He had wet his own bed and then climbed into ours. Even thinking about this now makes me feel awful, because it wasn't his fault, but the commotion of me jumping up and throwing the covers back woke the baby, whose cot was still in our room (and who had been up half the bloody night already). Upon realizing it was Saturday, that *this* was my weekend, I flipped out. I was calm enough to give the toddler a cuddle, put him under the shower and tell him it didn't matter *at all* that his bed was sopping wet and so was ours (I've developed an Oscar-winning smiley mum face). I was calm enough to take him downstairs and put some cartoons on and ask if he wanted Rice Krispies while James fruitlessly tried to get the now-savage baby back to sleep upstairs. But I had lost it. As I stomped back into our bedroom, deliberately slamming the door, I stripped the bedsheets and shouted (above the crying), "I wish we'd never had kids. What a mistake! *A mistake! Happy fucking Saturday!*" I later cried, because I've never truly wished we hadn't had kids at all. I just wished in that moment that one of our beds could have remained piss free and that our weekend lie-in had extended beyond five a.m.

Generally, I recognize that such outbursts are irrational. They are momentary, and not a reflection of my true feelings. *I didn't really mean it.* So I try not to beat myself up about them. But, in the grander scheme of all the thoughts and feelings I've come to regret, there is one that was less heat of the moment and more deep-rooted. One that lingered. A feeling I am not proud of. A feeling I regret having but am sharing because I promised I'd give you my honest account of motherhood.

At our twenty-week scan for baby number two, I lay with my tummy smothered in jelly and once again felt the butter-flies and slightly anxious knotty feeling that something might be wrong. Baby two might not be healthy. They do, after all, call it the "anomaly scan," and I'm sure all parents have a pang of desperate hope that everything remains anomaly free. We had one healthy child at home already. Our beautiful destroyer of peace, Hurricane Henry. All anybody would wish for would be an equally healthy sibling. Right? Well, I did wish for that. But I also wished for something else. Something seemingly far less important but which became all-consuming in the run-up to that scan.

I wished for a girl. I *wanted* a girl.

And when the moment of truth presented itself, it was clear to see that this wasn't to be. There wasn't any searching be-tween the baby's legs at this scan. Half the bloody screen was willy and balls at one point. We had been blessed with a second son, and all was well. We were so very, very lucky.

And yet I cried.

Not at first. At first, I delighted in the healthy-baby news and laughed at the obvious gender identification. Another little rascal like my Henry. *Really nice for him to have a little brother.*

But outside the hospital, I burst into tears. And more tears came later that afternoon, and later still in bed. I felt huge disappointment that we were having a second boy. I also felt like the world's worst mother—how pathetic and selfish of me to be disappointed. I was *so* angry at myself for reacting that way. What a dick. I'd always been baffled at those people you read about who keep trying for more children until they get one of the gender they have been longing for. The kind of stories that lend themselves to Channel 5 documentaries (*Twenty-Five Sons and Still Breeding*, or similar—although I'd absolutely tune in and watch that, to be fair). I just didn't believe that "gender disappointment" was a thing—surely nobody could be *disappointed*?

I truly never thought I would have a *preference*. I would just be grateful if we could have a healthy family. And yet there I was, with a funny feeling in my chest that wasn't pregnancy heartburn. My head was frantically trying to churn out rational thoughts to counteract this (we're blessed to be able to have children; he's *healthy*; we should be celebrating; get a grip, woman). I desperately wanted to snap out of it, to erase all feelings of disappointment. But you genuinely cannot help how you feel and, at the time, that is how I felt.

Well, I am now the proud owner of two boys and, though it's a bloody cliché to say you can't imagine life any other way, I genuinely can't imagine life any other way. When Jude smiles at me or chuckles at my dodgy rendition of "The Wheels on the Bus," I get a pang of guilt about the tears I shed in the hospital car park that day (and later that week, and much later still, when I found out my best friend was having a girl . . . yes, I know; absolutely ridiculous). I am now so content with my two boys it would be easy for me to deny I ever felt such disappointment, to laugh it off and forget about it. To delete my postscan blog post and erase that sentiment forever. But, now that I've had more than a year to reflect on those feelings, I have come to terms with them. It makes sense to me now in a way it did not at the time (though I was fat and hormonal then, so not a lot made sense).

I've realized that the disappointment I felt at the news that baby two was to be a boy was not at all rooted in not wanting another boy. I had spent two years with my glorious Henry and, despite finding motherhood immeasurably hard (*immeasurably*, I tell you), I was remarkably fond of our mother-son bond. There was something special about the thought of two boys. Brothers. I still like saying "my boys" now (and even include James in this, when he's behaving).

But back then I just felt a temporary (albeit overwhelming) sense of sadness that I would not have a daughter. Growing up as one of two girls, I had always imagined having daughters. I dreamed of spa breaks and shopping trips and chats about boyfriends. I am sure that losing my mum when I was fifteen heightened this sense of longing to have a daughter of my own. I wanted to re-create the memories I still hold so dearly. Bra shopping in M&S for that 28AA trainer bra we both knew I didn't need but was nevertheless essential to avoid the social suicide of being discovered braless while getting changed for PE. Singing in the kitchen to Eternal featuring BeBe Winans's "I Wanna Be the Only One" and acting out "protect you from the rain" with raindrop fingertips like total loons. The breakthrough of being allowed a Collection 2000 eyeshadow palette for Christmas following years of being told, "It will make you look like a tart." Despite never having been a particularly girly girl, I really cherished all that stuff—even more so when I realized how seriously ill Mum was getting. I think I clung on to the typical mother-daughter chats about starting my period and not squeezing spots because I knew they would soon be taken from me. My dad has done (and continues to do) an unbelievable job, supporting me throughout all the crucial life moments, and I am so very lucky to have him. But it has still proved heartbreakingly sad to go through all the "big stuff"—falling in love with James, getting married, becoming a mum—without having my own mum there to share any of it. I think my imaginary daughters were partly born from the promise to myself that I *would* be there for chats about going on the Pill and for wedding-dress shopping. It was such a clear future snapshot, maybe I had just never imagined an alternative. An alternative which, despite being fabulous in its own right, required me to let go of all I had imagined before.

I knew we wouldn't be one of those couples who keep on trying—we wanted two children, and we were lucky enough to have two children; they would be our lot, thank you and good night. My "gender disappointment" was not related to anything other than my realization during that trip to the Royal Devon and Exeter that I would never have a girl. It was like mourning an idea I'd had in my head for twenty-seven years that I now knew would never come to pass. I really hope saying so is not unfair to my boys and that one day they will understand. Because saying "I would have liked a girl" is not saying I didn't want boys. My dad often joked that he would have liked a son and, as his second daughter, that nugget of information never lessened my sense of self-worth. We used to laugh at him: oh, how outnumbered he was! We knew he loved us unconditionally, just as I love my boys. Just as they outnumber me.

There are always going to be times when I ponder the benefits of having a girl. Like the times I bypass all the pretty clothes and head straight for the jeans, T-shirts and trainers again. Sigh. The times when, despite my best efforts to promote the Let Toys Be Toys message (by buying dollhouses and kitchens), my boys still favor the so-called "boys' toys." My life is Ninja Turtles and Star Wars and, no, neither of my sons likes my suggestion of sitting down nicely to do a puzzle because they would rather pretend to shoot me while hanging off the back of the sofa. I have yet to meet girls who obsess over all things poo, bum, underpants and fart related as much as little boys do. Not once have I witnessed my niece, or any of my friends' lovely girls, shout, "Farty farty bum bum knickers *on your head*!" from the top of a climbing frame. Yet, secretly, I laugh at this humor and, despite my dislike of gender stereotyping, I smile at observations from strangers that they are "proper little boys" (while outwardly having a stern word about the "bum bum underpants" shouting, obviously).

Boys and girls *are* very different and—I'm not going to lie—one of each would have been nice: I always said "one of each" was like the Holy Grail; to achieve it is to hit the jackpot. And yet I've come to realize that "two of the same" is a stupid thing to say because no two children are the same. The willy-and-balls identification at the scan is, so far, the biggest similarity my boys have shared; they are chalk and cheese personality-wise. We don't have two of the *same* at all.

A full year after blogging honestly about that twenty-week scan, I'm surprised that I still receive messages about it. From the mum who imagined she would have a houseful of boys and went on to have three girls. The mum who "just knew" she was having a girl then had a pang of disappointment when "she" came out with a willy. The mum who had one of each and secretly felt awful that she was so relieved, guilty that she would have cried if it had gone any other way. The common thread throughout was that none of them had ever shared these feelings. Maybe it's just not something we are allowed to say. But it's too late for me to put the cat back in the bag.

I still feel like a prize twit for how I reacted. The kind of stupid you feel when you have a drunken argument and then wish you could take it back. I wish I hadn't shed those tears. I wish I could have behaved like all the other parents, who really don't mind either way. It all seems so bloody irrelevant now, but I can tell you it was a very real feeling at the time. It shocked me. Maybe it is better to allow yourself to "have a moment" rather than bottling up the unsaid. When people declare, "You can't say that!" what they really mean is, "You can think it, but you mustn't say it." I don't think keeping thoughts to yourself makes them any less real.

My boys will undoubtedly wind me up more in the coming years, knowing I once longed for a girl. I hope they know that what I longed for most of all was a family. And a family I have got. I'm sure there will be days when I would pay good money to swap Batman role-play and stinky-poo-poo-bum conversations for princess parties and hair plaiting (though if she were anything like me, any daughter of mine would probably have preferred Batman anyway). Mostly, I think I will feel contentment when I'm picking up my boys' trainers and hoodies, contentment that they are both healthy. Having two boys has proved pretty special already, and this is only the beginning. I truly am happy with my lot. If only they would fart a bit less.

"When I was pregnant with my second child and I asked my daughter whether she would be having a brother or a sister, her reply was, always, 'a bugger.' Quite an accurate description of her brother, as it turned out."

EMMA, TAUNTON

Second-Child Shortcuts

"WE'LL TREAT THEM both the same," we said, with the sincerest of intentions. We were painting our (then unnamed) second bump's nursery and mulling over the unfortunate tendency we'd witnessed in other families to fuss massively over their firstborn and leave the second child to be, well, just a bit *unfussed*.

Not us. We would treat our second baby-boy bundle exactly the same as we had our first. Deep down, I think we knew this was a lie even then.

Not a sneaky, malicious lie, but a lie rooted in the most genuine of intentions. The truth was, as James and I merrily glossed the skirting boards and chatted about bump number two, we discovered we both felt a kind of protective appreciation for his second-child status. We had a connection. As second children ourselves, each with an older sibling of the same sex, we had been brought up knowing the second-child drill.

Not that being the second child has been a bad thing—we haven't suffered in any way because of it. It's definitely *not* as if I still hold a grudge that my parents took my sister to Brownies and dance lessons but didn't bother taking me to either; or that my dad could never remember my date of birth so used to offer my sister's as the default. Scarred for life. (Just kidding, Dad, I know I'm your favorite. Bet you can't remember the year, though.)

All right, so we've fared just fine as second children, but we also appreciate the inescapable reality of life with an older sibling.

Who always does everything first.

Whose hand-me-downs we were forced to wear years later.

Who always has the bigger bloody room.

The writing (or, in this case, painting) was very much on the wall of Jude's (50 percent smaller than Henry's) nursery as we decorated it that day.

Our little fetus had already been allocated the box room.

It had begun.

I'm glad we voiced our determination to treat our babies the same (the will was there, Jude), but we were stupid to state this intention *before* we had experienced the reality of a toddler-and-baby combo. It was wrong (and naive) of me to scorn other parents from afar for the lack of fuss they gave their second child compared with their first. I just didn't get it.

Now I'm living with the at-times-impossible task of juggling all that nice baby fuss and attention with answering to my other child's commands as he launches himself off the sofa, shouting, "You be Chewie, Mummy. *Do the voice!*" (I do a pretty top-notch Chewbacca impression, it has to be said.) So I really wish I could say I had iMessaged James with the moment Jude clapped for the first time (as I'm confident I did for Henry), but the truth is I don't know when that happened. I probably missed it while I was making a cheese sandwich and/or putting away the pens and pencils that provided entertainment for all of fifteen seconds while sighing, "Can everybody just calm *down* a bit?"

Jude has not been treated the same as Henry was, but I don't really feel all that bad because, despite claiming we hadn't overindulged Henry, I have since realized that much of what we practiced the first time around was unnecessary. In many ways, I much *prefer* my second-child parenting behaviors. Less anal, less worrisome, less superfluous (such a great word, "superfluous"—I'm not sure I've ever used it before; I hope my editor lets me keep it).

I'm not saying we have been *slack* second time around, but we have definitely been more relaxed. And by "relaxed," I mostly mean we've been too preoccupied to fuss.

In our first few months of parenting Henry we expressed grave concern at every slightly damp spot on his sleepsuit shoulder. We analyzed every nappy noise and, where there was doubt, changed him anyway. Even at three a.m., when he had drifted back to sleep, we awoke him from his slumber to investigate (because a screaming baby was *obviously* less of an issue than the risk of a wet fart). We used to change him into a new

Babygro if there was the slightest of marks on the old one. We clearly had too much time on our hands. Or too much surplus space in the washing machine.

With Jude, "gray area" nappy noises are ignored unless we can smell something (and even then, in the sleep-deprived early hours, I have been known to turn a blind eye, and ear, and nose). Our Babygro-changing rule these days is simple: if it is dry and largely stain free, it stays put. Admittedly, we reached a new parenting low when Jude was around four months old and we used the hair dryer to give the sicky, wet shoulder patch a quick blast. While he was still in the Babygro. But it *was* the cool setting and babies *like* white noise, and I think I had probably been crying and James thought it best just to get the kids to bed sharpish. (I'm definitely not recommending this as an approach to laundry, just so we're clear.)

Arguably, the biggest change between the treatments of our boys as babies has been the rules. You know, all the stuff you're supposed to do. Or not do.

With Henry: "I don't really want to introduce him to unhealthy food at all. There's really no need, is there?"

With Jude: "What's that on his chin? Oh, wait, I think it's relish from your Big Mac."

With Henry: "Let's give him another bath and a little massage with some of that nice lavender stuff."

With Jude: "Do you think his neck smells a bit cheesy? Pass me a wipe. I'll give him a proper wash tomorrow."

With Henry: "We need to buy some more books. I'm running out of stories for the bedtime feed!"

With Jude: "Shit, he's six months old and I haven't read to him yet."

As a first-time mum, I agonized over the feed/sleep routine. ("He can't nap now, it's five thirty p.m.! Do you think Gina Ford would let this happen?!") Some days, I paced the living room for up to an hour to "stretch out the feeds" in pursuit of the target gap between them.

Second time around, I just wouldn't have dreamed of getting myself in a state over it. In fact, one time when I was feeling quite poorly, I breastfed Jude pretty much every time he moved. There was no stretching out of feeds that day. I had lost all regard for the time of his last feed and chose instead to feed him into a milk stupor because I was also having to supervise my toddler's living-room reenactment of the Great Fire of Pontypandy. There were other times, too, in those early months when I gave baby Jude an arguably unnecessary top-up feed and let him nap way later than was sensible just so I could do the washing. And watch *Made in Chelsea*.

Then there's all the material stuff, where we've definitely failed at equality. For Henry's first Christmas we overspent. We bought him an array of toys and clothes that he would "grow into" and sat unwrapping them for him, saying, "Wow, do you like your new toy, darling?" as he disinterestedly crawled off to find a candle to chew or a patio door to lick. Jude was just fifteen weeks old for his first Christmas and, as he wasn't really sitting up and had no interest even in the wrapping paper, we decided we'd buy him just a couple of token gifts. A small part of me felt like I was letting him down that morning, but a bigger part of me knew he didn't need a gigantic stocking. I hope we've made up for it since.

So, when you read this, Jude, my little pudding face, I hope you accept an apology on behalf of your dad and me, who, despite our best intentions, have already failed miserably at treating you the same as your brother.

The following is for you, and only you (written after I suffered a second-child-guilt meltdown):

To my little Ginger Biscuit,

I'm writing to the Future You to say sorry.

Sorry that I haven't been religiously recording your milestones in your "Baby's First Year" keepsake book. I kind of wish I hadn't bought one because all the gaps remind me I have no idea when you started to do stuff. ("My first tooth came on . . ." Good question. "The outfit I wore home from hospital was . . ." Erm . . . well, it was that, um . . . I don't know. Literally no idea.)

I'm sorry I've neglected to get things on video. Somewhere on the computer you'll find a video of the day Henry crawled for the first time and I recorded one of those cringey voiceovers ("September 2012, and he's on the move! Watch out, ladies!" [chuckles at own funniness]).

I forgot to get a video of your early crawling.

I forgot to get a video of you sitting and clapping.

In fact—where the hell are all your baby videos? It's like one day you were a crinkly newborn and the next you were cruising the furniture and biting things with teeth; teeth I definitely forgot to record in that bloody book.

I doubt you will ever need to know the date you first rolled over, or the date of your first beach trip, or what your favorite puree was during weaning.* But if you ever do want to know these things I will probably scratch my head trying to remember and the answer will be a guess. I'm sorry about that.

I hope these things won't matter to you. Because it's true I have been a bit less attentive. It's true I haven't shared as many baby pictures of you on Facebook (because there just aren't as many baby pictures of you). It's true I make that startled face when people ask me questions I really should know the answer to.

But I love you just the same.

I love you because you are not the same. You are special for all of your own quirks and I bloody love the bones of you.

I hope you know that although it may seem like I am always putting your brother first, you are just as important. It's just that when you were very small he was the one charging around shouting, the one asking me why the roadkill on the road had to die, the one needing poos at inconvenient times—he was three years old and demanded my time. I never had the chance to take you to baby massage and rotate your small, oily legs while singing about Daisy, Daisy, and the bicycle made for two.

In the first year of your life we actually spent very little time just us two, but your turn will come, my little potato head. Henry is going to school this year, and when he does you can rest assured you will not be spending the day sitting in the Jumperoo or sucking a bread stick.

---

*You didn't actually have purees. Not homemade ones like I blitzed in the blender for your brother, anyway. You survived on manufactured jars and pouches. I'm sorry about that, too.

Being second born does not mean you are second best.

It just means you are one of two, and Mummy is finding that doing the best by everyone is a challenge.

I love you forever and ever, my Angel Plum Plums.

Mum xx

P.S. All the best people are born second.

Don't tell your brother.

Part Four

THE DAILY GRIND

"Staying at home all day
is almost always a *terrible* idea."

SAHMs, I Salute You

"NICE GIG if you can get it," I once said about stay-at-home mums. "I'm sure we'd all love to be at home all day." How nice it must be never to get that Monday-morning feeling, to plan your week around playdates and park trips and fucking babyccinos in Costa. What a life!

I take it all back.

I had no idea. No bloody idea. If you are reading this and you are a SAHM (stay-at-home mum—not a term I like, by the way, but one that has stuck), you should know that right now I am doing that embarrassing "we're not worthy" gesture people do to demonstrate admiration and respect. You deserve some recognition here. You deserve an apology from dimwits like me who once thought you had it easy. I hadn't lived it. *I didn't know.*

I know now. Turns out being at home and in charge of small people day in, day out is not quite the easy life I'd imagined. And when I say it's not *quite* as easy, I mean it turned out to be some serious mind-messing shit that I was *not* prepared for.

I know several mums who have taken the best part of a year off on maternity leave. I didn't even reach a year for both maternity leaves put together. The second time, I cut my pre-agreed maternity leave (of six months) short to just five after e-mailing my boss to ask if I could come back early. I wasn't coping all that well at home. I couldn't hack it. I couldn't hack being at home all day every day (every week, every month).

I have been asked a few times, "What's so hard about it, then?" and it's a good question. But where do I start?

I'm not sure there's any *one* thing about staying at home I can't cope with. Perhaps that's why I thought it would be easy. Because, taken by themselves, keeping up with the housework and calming a grizzly baby and nipping to the shop do not sound unmanageable. Sometimes, I manage these things just fine.

But the culmination of a whole host of factors in a day spent at home with small people is a mental boiling point unlike any work stress I've ever experienced.

It's the whining. Jesus Christ, the whining! Hour upon hour of slightly whiny noises intermingled with less regular but more severe bouts of crying or screaming.

It's not being able to complete any task successfully without interruptions. Some days, all I want to do is hang out the wet washing from two days ago (which is smelling so moldy I'm considering rewashing it), or eat one piece of toast before my child declares himself to be "starving" and I find myself handing him his second breakfast after I've eaten half of one crust. Sometimes, as I battle with bumped heads ("For God's sake, what did I say about using the sofa as a slide!") and the daily protests about putting pants/coats/shoes on, I realize I am pinning the *entire* success of my day on at least one of my children having a nap.

And then there's the monotony. I know it's not socially acceptable for mums to say they find motherhood boring, but, *sometimes, I find motherhood boring.* That's not to say my kids are boring—far from it, they amaze and entertain me every single day. But the nap routines and chores and repeats of *Fireman Sam* before the seventeenth weekly trip to the park can on occasion seem just a bit dull. I wish I didn't feel that way, but I do. I suspect I am not alone.

SAHMs deserve a bloody Pride of Britain award for patience. Sure, everybody loses patience at times (stuck in traffic/ on the phone to the tax office/trying to assemble flat-pack toy storage/dealing with knobheads in general), but I never felt overwhelming surges of *impatience* until I started spending full days at home with small people. Patience-testing moments for me during a day at home include:

- Henry having an "I will/I won't" tantrum. If you've never played this game with a three-year-old, let me tell you, it's a real treat. You ask the child to do something (like go for a wee before you leave the house) and the child point-blank refuses ("I won't"). The consequence of this is a warning, followed by the time-out chair, where he screams, *"I will! I will! I will!"* until you remove him from said chair and steer him toward the loo. Where he forgets the preceding ten minutes and shouts, *"I won't!"* and another piece of your soul is destroyed.

- The same level of frenzied rage because I won't let him go to the *one* shop he so desperately wants to go to. More often than not, this will be somewhere totally random. Like Vision Express.

- Jude crying because he wants a yogurt, then crying some more because he doesn't want a yogurt. Basically, it's the yogurt's fault. Bastard inconsiderate yogurt.

- As above, but substitute "Heinz biscotti" for "yogurt."

- Henry walking deliberately sloooowwlyyy back from town. Not because his little legs are tired but because I've made the mistake of telling him we need to get back to feed his brother. Cue a pointless "Let's have a race!" attempt from me (he's not daft) followed by the obligatory *"I'm not going to tell you again"* (as I tell him again).

- Teething (enough said).

- Both boys whining for forty minutes in the car, at a volume just above the Disney song that's on repeat. A patient mum would recognize that her children are just overtired and sing along to distract them. She would certainly not resort to underbreath swearing.

I kidded myself for a while that if I hadn't been so keen to return to work and rejoin the career ladder, I would have enjoyed devoting more of those months to full-time motherhood. I think I may even have used that line once or twice ("It's a shame I can't have more time off, but I need to get back to work"). It wasn't a shame. Returning to work was the easy option for me—even the most testing of work days seemed somehow easier than being at home. At times, it feels like a holiday.

I have also spoken to *so* many mums via the blog who have admitted that, for a whole host of reasons, work feels like a holiday for them, too. It's a holiday, they've explained, because when you're at work:

- You can drink a cup of tea without having to scream, *"Watch my tea. Watch my tea!"* as a small person toddles precariously close to it.
- Your lunch is *your* lunch. It is not stolen. Or sneezed on. You don't have to hide behind the fridge door pretending to look for a yogurt while secretly stuffing your face with a cookie.
- You aren't followed to the loo or watched while you are on it.
- You get to wear something that doesn't have vomit crust on the sleeve. Okay, sometimes you will still have something crusty on your sleeve (although you will be surprised at your depths of resourcefulness in the face of adversity—the old wet-wipe-and-Febreze garment freshen-up is surprisingly effective). I wore a proper blouse and statement necklace to a meeting recently and kept playing with the necklace until somebody commented, "I like

your necklace." (I can't wear it at home because the baby tries to asphyxiate me with his grabby hands.)

- Nobody in the office climbs all over you (unless you want them to, which is, of course, your business). You won't feel the need to sit at the bottom of the stairs with your fingers in your ears, shouting, "*Time-out!* Mummy's having a *time-out!*"
- You can converse all day with adults about *Strictly Come Dancing*, diets and affairs. ("She *didn't!* So she wasn't at Zumba?")
- You can go for a walk on your lunch/coffee break. Alone. *Without carrying a bag.*

Admittedly, these benefits of a day at work don't apply to all jobs. Teachers, child minders, nursery workers and the like don't get a sabbatical from the chorus of screaming children (busman's holiday right there), and not everybody has time to enjoy a hot cup of tea at work. That said, I have had several messages from parents with extremely stressful day jobs (and some who do night shifts) saying that there are times when work still feels like a sabbatical compared to a day at home with their children. Perhaps a change is as good as a rest.

It's not all one-sided, of course—there are many less-appreciated benefits of being at home: not having to make small talk with people you don't really like, eating what you fancy without being silently judged by colleagues who are on the 5:2 diet, watching *Homes Under the Hammer*. Above all, simply spending time with your little ones is a privilege: being there for first steps and first words, for example. Despite my eagerness to get back to the office, both times, the end of my maternity leave still brought with it the realization that I would miss my children so much my heart would hurt. "Hurty heart," I call it. I'm pretty sure it's a medical condition.

I have, however, learned to accept hurty heart as part of my life these days, because I am sure my heart would hurt in a different way if I gave up work altogether. Besides, I've discovered firsthand that I'm not cut out for the alternative: I am not patient or resilient enough to cope at home every day.

SAHMs, I truly do salute you.

"I'm a nurse and a twelve-hour shift in intensive care with monitors and ventilator alarms going off, delirious patients and patients with profuse diarrhea is like annual leave compared to fourteen-month-old twins."

JANINE, SHREWSBURY

Sod's Law for Parents

HERE ARE SOME "bloody typical" moments guaranteed to happen at some point in your parenting life:

Bumping into somebody you've not seen for ages when you look like shit, accompanied by snotty, unruly children ("Yes, these are mine . . .")
Sod's Law states that if said someone is an ex-boyfriend (or ex-girlfriend), you will look exceptionally shit. Like a dog's dinner after it has been rained on.

This law is particularly painful if you knew that person in your life pre-kids, because it's possible they will hold a memory of your tamed eyebrows and/or your legs minus leggings. If this chance encounter happens in the supermarket, every inch of your body will scream at you to dive headfirst into the lettuces. But you cannot abandon a trolley laden with kids, so you will nod, and say, "Hi, you all right? Yeah, good, thanks. You?" while wanting to die.

The one day you do make an effort (wrestle into skinny jeans/slap on some BB cream and lip balm), there will be no such old-flame encounter.

The zip on the Grobag/snowsuit/pram hood breaking or getting stuck mid-baby-meltdown

Or, as we like to say in our house, when the baby has "gone savage." The zip, etc., will never break or get stuck when your baby is in a good mood, it's always when his world is ending and/or you are in a rush. You will be left trying to fix a broken zip underneath the chin of a crying and kicking, beetroot-faced baby. Upon experiencing such zip breakage, I challenge you not to shout, "You good-for-nothing piece of shit! I'm writing to the manufacturer to complain!" (You will never actually get round to this.)

Your children "sleeping in" on the days you need them to get up

Saturday morning with nowhere to be? Oh, they're awake at four a.m., jumping on the bed and shouting, "Bundle!" and telling you they have a snotty nose. And can they watch *Ben 10*?

But when the Thursday six a.m. alarm goes off for the child minder run . . . they are in a sleep coma. What is that about?

It also goes without saying that the first time the baby sleeps through the night, the otherwise sleep-trained toddler will wake at least twice. That's a rule.

NOWOs (Naps of Wasted Opportunity)

You can be driving for an hour, hoping your child will drop off so you can listen to the radio in peace, but he will maintain a constant whine until you are five minutes from home. You will then find yourself sitting in the car outside your house, drinking in the silence while at the same time thinking, This is another sodding NOWO. If he just napped in his goddamn bed you could put some washing out. And watch *Judge Rinder.*

And when he does have a nap in his cot or bed? Well, either the sound of the kettle boiling will serve as an alarm clock or, just as you do sit down with that cuppa, the doorbell rings and half your family turns up. "No, we're not up to anything," you'll tell them. While mourning that lost moment of unexploited peace and quiet.

The Sod's Law timing of naps extends to babies at important events or functions. My best friend, when recently debriefing me via WhatsApp on the two weddings and a funeral she had been to with her small baby, reflected, "She managed to sleep soundly until the exact moment the bride/coffin arrived. It's like she could smell the importance." They just know.

The baby choosing to poo at inconvenient times

You will spend a ridiculous amount of your life muttering, "For fuck's sake!" while angrily getting another nappy out (usually when you have only just changed the previous one, as babies seem to love nothing more than pooing in a brand-new nappy). For this reason, you must allow at least a forty-minute margin of error in any target house-departure time. Of course, when you finally are all out of the door (and the small people are strapped into car seats), he will somehow manage to squeeze another one out. Or be sick. At this point, you will deny all knowledge and drive to Sainsbury's. Other Sod's Law poo timings include the moment your food arrives in a restaurant, the moment you are called in to see the doctor and the moment you are anywhere without wipes. I know it is pretty inconceivable ever to be anywhere without wipes (even without the kids; bloody love a wipe, me), but one time this did happen to me. Loo paper does *not* rectify the aftermath of a shit explosion in Pizza Hut.

A family bug striking when you have a night out planned

Your *one night* of freedom will die a germy death as one or all of the family start vomiting before you've even had the chance to dry-shampoo your hair. Probably for the best, as you are all out of Febreze for those jeans.

The same lurgy fate will also strike on the blue moon when you have managed to secure a babysitter and just as you head off on holiday. Splendid.

Bachelorette parties, thirtieth birthday parties and general organized fun activities occurring when you are eight months pregnant

If you stay at home, you will sit on the sofa drinking raspberry-leaf tea and watching *Strictly*, feeling like you are missing out. If you go, you will be fat, sweaty and sober (and will have paid for the privilege). There is no winner here (except everybody else, who gain a designated driver). If the nonpregnant you does brave a G&T (or four), your children will almost certainly be up half the night. Eight-month sleep regression? How about the "Mummy and Daddy tried to enjoy a normal adult evening, the stupid buggers!" sleep regression?

I'm telling you: they just know.

And the biggest and soddiest law of all . . .

Your children behaving impeccably for others

Perhaps less Sod's Law and more Fuck My Luck, this one. Not FML that your child behaves nicely, because, of course, good behavior is welcomed with open arms. Rather, the injustice lies in the fact that your child will appear to save this exemplary behavior for everybody else. You will get the shitty end of the stick, the end with the tantrums and the crying and the sometimes actually exploding shit.

"He's been such a good boy, a total dream!" people would tell me after looking after Henry.

"Sorry, what?"

I'd let it sink in for a moment.

A total fucking dream.

Surely he wasn't a dream when he refused point-blank to sit in the pram and threw his bottle in the road on purpose and deliberately banged his head on the table because his sandwiches were not Just So? When he wouldn't nap but then cried all day because he was so tired from not napping? When he wouldn't let you change his nappy, instead kicking and screaming and trying to roll over as if you were torturing him when actually you were just trying to wipe up the poo, the poo that had now spread to all the places he'd rolled?

"He didn't do any of those things with us."

"Right," I'd say, while thinking, "Well, that's just bloody marvelous." I initially concluded (much the same as always) that it must just be me. He must be picking up on my unmumsiness and preying on my moments of nappy-changing incompetence, perhaps living in hope of securing a bag of Quavers. He acted up on the days I had him because he knew I was an accident of motherhood.

But a few years (and another baby) later, I've started to accept that, for most of us, that's just how it is.

Parents simply get the worst of it.

I know for certain I am not alone in this; the hilarious tales I've received from other parents have reaffirmed this. Like the time a dad I'd met told me that at one stage, he and his wife were genuinely convinced that their son had a vendetta against them. Granny and Grandad reported he'd been "good as gold," and staff at the nursery said how easy he was to look after. This was a conspiracy, he told me, because at home their son was the toddler version of Kevin. From *We Need to Talk About Kevin*.

Oh, how I laughed as he told me all about toddler Kevin, but, amidst the humor, I could sense their genuine concern, coupled with their incredulity that the same boy could be a total shit with them and an absolute angel with others.

Mostly, I think we should remember it's not a true FML moment at all and just be thankful that our children are behaving. The fact that my boys are "an absolute dream" most of the time means people are happy to look after them. The alternative doesn't bear thinking about . . .

However, in the spirit of honesty, I'll admit (and it's not something I'm proud of) that there have been times when I have found myself almost *willing* my children to behave badly for somebody else. Longing for somebody else to say, "Jesus, they were hard work today!" so I can return a "welcome to my world" shrug and relish the corroboration of my story. Maybe I just need to feel validated in my assertion that it's all so bloody hard.

Have I mentioned that yet? ☺

Get Out, Get Out, Wherever You Are

LOOKING BACK at some of the absolute worst days I've had as a parent, days I have felt completely lost, frustrated and bored (and subsequently guilty about feeling lost, frustrated and bored), there is definitely a pattern regarding the nature of the day I've had and what I have been doing.

It took me a good year or so to recognize that on these days (those "I hate every minute of this!" days), I have usually spent most, if not all, of my day at home.

I haven't ventured out.

As a new mum, I regularly made the mistake of thinking I would find a day at home *easier*. Even with baby Henry, when I had one less child to wrestle in and out of the car, I regularly came to the conclusion that hanging out in the living room would be far less hassle, not least because getting out of the house at a reasonable time is a massive ball-ache when you have small children. You said you'd meet your friend at "elev-enish" and it's already twelve thirty and the baby's due his lunch soon, and if you get there much after one o'clock it'll be time for his nap, so there's just no point in going . . .

There have been times when, in my tired and slightly deli-cate state, I have also felt that a day at home would be the safer option.

Much less risky.

No observable tantrums, no baby vomiting over a stranger in Starbucks (yes, that happened once), no embarrassing spec-tacle as you battle to get your child (who has contorted his body into a floorboard) back into the pram, shamefully resort-ing to bribing him with a Freddo while resisting the urge to shout, "I know he's been shrieking for half an hour and doesn't deserve a treat, but I don't know how to do it without the sod-ding chocolate frog!" (while crying). Venturing out could lead to all of these things. It's best not to chance it, right?

Wrong, I think, actually.

I've come to realize that staying at home all day is almost always a *terrible* idea.

When I weigh up the hundreds of days I've spent at home versus the hundreds of days I've spent out and about, there is no doubt that the latter have been easier. Despite the obvious challenges attached to leaving the house (like packing a moun-tain of stuff, risking the meltdowns and worrying about the weather), nothing is *mentally* as tough as confinement in the house with small people.

I always have this vision that our "home days" will be cozy and snuggly and full of Fun Mum craft activities, but the reality of a whole day at home is more often than not just a bit shit. I can usually be found running around trying to sort out endless piles of washing while supervising the baby's choice of teether ("Not the phone charger—Henry, take the charger out of his mouth!"), standing by for bum-wiping duties and reboiling the kettle for the umpteenth time.

When I do sit down with a probably tepid drink somebody is guaranteed to cry.

A day at home just feels soooooo loooooooooooooooooooong.

Each minute feels like four when you are trying to hold a conversation (about the yogurt raisins you have just found posted behind the radiator) over the background hum of the Early Learning Centre Lights and Sounds Keyboard in Demo Mode.

Fun Mum crafts are a fate worse than death—usually, a glittery and gluey fate—where I feel the rage boiling in me because my child specifically requested "five paints and five brushes," but now that I've set up the sodding paint station he only wants to use a highlighter pen (*my* highlighter pen, one of only two surviving "work pens" I have to my name).

I have usually already lost the plot by the time *This Morning* starts. I don't even get to watch Schofe the Silver Fox interview somebody with two penises because Henry starts complaining that he wants to watch *his* telly and I realize the children are at risk of Square Eyes, if there is such a thing, so I turn it off.

Some days, I start preparing lunch at 11:15 because, once lunch is over, it's officially the afternoon, isn't it? I know that's bloody stupid logic and, in reality, I'm just dragging out the afternoon. But at least "after lunch" sounds nearer to Daddy Rescue Time, nearer to the pajamas, milk, book, bed sequence otherwise known as the "home straight." I always feel awful for wishing the time away when I should be appreciating each moment (hello again, Mum Guilt), but clock-watching is an easy habit to fall into when you are bouncing off the same four walls you bounced off the day before, and the day before, and . . .

On the days James has asked, "How was your day, babe?" and I've replied, "It was shit. I hate being at home. I hate maternity leave. I hate every minute of it," I can almost guarantee I have been at home all day. By the same token, I know when I've replied, "Pretty good, actually!" the boys and I have almost always been up to something. We have *been somewhere*.

The crazy thing is, when I say "somewhere," I literally mean *anywhere* that isn't our house. I'm not just talking about libraries and baby groups and playdates at other people's houses (though all of these have their merits). I'm talking about garden centers and shopping centers. The hours of fun there are to be had exploring the "small animal zoo" (aka Pets at Home) and running riot in the hedging-plants section of the garden center! We have enjoyed outings to some bloody random places—and I mean properly enjoyed; this isn't even sarcastic. For ages, Henry kept asking if we could go back to "the orange shop," and I couldn't for the life of me work out what he meant.

"The orange shop with the playhouses," he clarified.

By "playhouses," he meant sheds.

He was talking about the hardware store B&Q.

So, sometimes, we go to B&Q. Not a weekend outing to pick up a new drill bit or some white latex paint but a midweek excursion, *something to do* ("Shall we go to B&Q, Henry?" "*Yayyyyyyy!*"), and we look at the sheds (occasionally, they have genuine playhouses, too) and I push Jude around in the trolley and we wave at people picking up drill bits and white latex paint . . . Yes, I realize this whole admission about how we get our kicks in B&Q makes me sound like a total fruit loop, but, the truth is, it passes the time. And after parking up, having a traipse around, standing looking at electric fires (family tradition) and then going home again, sometimes a whole hour and a half has passed where nobody cried.

And that, I think, is the whole purpose of an excursion outside the house: it breaks the day up into manageable chunks. Even a trip to the sodding dentist breaks the day up. Where we go, what we do, doesn't really matter—it's simply a bonus if it's time we would otherwise have spent indoors with me getting cross, silently wishing the hours until Daddy Rescue Time would arrive.

It's all about a much-needed change of scene—the kids need it and, Lord knows, I need it. Mostly, I need an incentive to get out of my dressing gown, in which I have been known to unhappily fester all day.

I occasionally have moments when I wake up tempted by a Snuggly Home Day, but nowadays, when I hear myself say, "We'll just have a day at home today, shall we, boys?" it triggers a wiser part of my brain to scream, "Awful idea, Mummy. Rethink it immediately." Unless one of us is really very poorly (and physically can't exit the house), I make sure we plan at least one outing or excursion every day. Every now and again, we go to Pets at Home and B&Q in the same day.

Those are the days I am winning at life.

(Yes, I, too, am finding it difficult to understand when browsing guinea pigs and DIY materials became a "win.")

"No one tells you about the shower of shit days. I reckon 60/40 [in favor of] shit."
JAE, GLASGOW

The Frustration of Toddlers

WHEN HENRY was a baby he used to stare quizzically at me from his bouncer, looking slightly disturbed by my one-way conversation. Maybe he was just a bit bored by the tenth round of peek-a-boo and was thinking, "Oh, God, not the old 'Where's Mummy gone?' charade again." Yep, she's behind the sicky muslin. What a surprise.

Besides the clapping and the row, row, rowing the bloody boat, you just can't *do* a lot by way of activities with babies, can you? I remember longing for Henry to get bigger so I could interact with him properly. You know, play proper games.

It's only now that he is *considerably* bigger (a preschooler, starting actual schooly school this year: arghhh) that the proper playing stage is starting to materialize. I'm welcoming it, too, because the interim toddler period of games and activities, though hilarious at times, has proved pretty testing. The truth is, you can't really play *games* with toddlers at all, though you'll have a bloody good bash at it.

So now that Jude is on the cusp of toddlerhood (lock up your toddling daughters!), I'm preparing myself all over again and, this time, I know (largely) what to expect.

If you're yet to reach this stage, here are a few upcoming highlights to look forward to:

Hide and Seek

Get your best poker face and annoying-parent voice ready (you *know* the one; if you don't, just go up an octave), because *your toddler will tell you where he is going to hide*. "I'll be under the table, Mummy." Excellent. Better still, after counting to ten, you will see him very obviously lying on the sofa with only his head concealed, with a cushion, giggling and/or farting with excitement, and the whole "No sign of him here!" charade will commence.

Initially quite amusing, the fun factor soon wears off as you "search" the living room for the blatantly visible (and sometimes sniffable) small person for the seventy-sixth time. Sigh.

From time to time, you can make this game work to your advantage by sending your small person upstairs to hide and counting to at least one hundred before periodically shouting, "Hmmmm, no sign of him in the kitchen!" or "Definitely not in this cupboard!" as you gaze at pictures of an old schoolfriend's wedding on Facebook. On a good day, this can buy you ten minutes to sort out the washing (or eat a KitKat

Chunky). On a really good day, your toddler will hide somewhere comfy and fall asleep by the time you get there.

Football

"I'll be Liverpool, Mummy. You be Chelsea." Superb. An actual game, at last. Goals are set up, the baby is relocated to the Jumperoo to avoid impact damage, you shimmy into position to "save" the shot that will never come close to the goal . . . and your toddler starts crying.

"Don't stop the ball, Mummy. *Mummy!* It has to *go in there.*" Your explanation of the whole point of the game falls on deaf ears until you no longer have any fucks to give about the point of the game and basically stand there complimenting the "goals" he scores in a keeperless net from a distance of five inches. This game has recently improved pretty dramatically for us, to the point that I can now pretend I am *trying* to save his shots (but still know better than to actually block one from entering the goal).

Frozen

In a game probably infiltrating houses worldwide after the 2013 chilly-themed Disney offering, your toddler will want to "act out" the film. I was actually pretty excited about the prospect of a bit of amateur dramatics before lunchtime. It had to be better than the excruciatingly pointless football.

"You be Anna, Mummy. I'm Elsa. I'll go behind that door."

Excellent. Act two, scene one commences . . .

Me: [coughs, ready to sing at the door] Do you want to build a snowman?

Toddler: *Yes, please!*

Face palm. He's seen it one hundred times and yet still lacks any comprehension of the main plot theme. I tried to explain how exasperating I found this episode to James one evening after work and, unsurprisingly, he laughed his head off at my annoyance about Disney plot comprehension. There I was, standing in the kitchen, becoming increasingly angry about our attempt at *Frozen* role-play until I heard myself say to my husband, with genuine concern, "She obviously *doesn't* want to build a bloody snowman. *That's the point.*"

And realized what my life had come to.

Anything Crafty

You can derive lots of hopeful intentions from Fun Mum Pinterest boards: there is something very *homey* about setting up drawing/painting/sticking and suchlike, especially when it's raining. But the absolute worst thing you can do when there's a toddler at large amidst crafting paraphernalia is have a target finished artwork in mind. Because it won't happen. And the urge to wail, "You're not doing it right!" can be overwhelming.

One time, I got out a whole host of fun crafty stuff to make some 3-D sheep (think pipe cleaners, cotton wool, sparkly card, even some googly eyes), and I was full of hope as my dining table morphed into the *Art Attack* desk. But, alas, in the end, Henry stuck the cotton wool on his fingers, the googly eyes to his chair and the pipe cleaners up his nose, leaving me to rustle up the fluffy cotton-wool sheep (which I then displayed in the kitchen with the byline "By Henry, aged 2").

I was only lying to myself. (But, naturally, I'll have to do the same for Jude's "aged 2" 3-D sheep creation this year; it's only fair.)

Cars

> "I hate playing 'cars.' Sigh. So I try to make it as interesting as possible for myself: 'Look, the car is driving to the kitchen. Oh, it's gone to the biscuit cupboard.'"
>
> DANI, SOUTHAMPTON

This game is pretty basic. It's also pretty dull. You get down on the floor and "drive" a tiny toy car while following the path of the toddler's tiny toy car. Sometimes this will be a race. You will be required to make annoying engine noises.

The only hard-and-fast rule is: you get the shittier car. And the second only hard-and-fast rule is: you never win.

Henry recently decided to make this game slightly more interesting when, during his second week of preschool, I had to pick him up early after he swallowed a wheel from one of said tiny toy cars in its entirety (no, I don't know if it "passed," just in case you're wondering). After debriefing him about the car-wheel-swallowing incident, I was at least comforted by the fact that he 100 percent did not willingly put the car wheel anywhere near his mouth. Definitely not.

"It flew in there, Mummy."

Of course it did, my little Pinocchio.

I'll be honest, it's not just "games" that prove interesting (do I mean that?) when you have a toddler at large. Hell no, that's just the start! There is *so much more* to look forward to . . . Here are my top reasons why toddlers are, in fact, tossers:

They call your bluff

At the park, when you threaten to leave ("Come *on*, it's time to go. I'll go without you—'*Bye, then!*'"), they shoot you a look which says, "You do that," and potter off back toward the slide. The little bastards. You then have to face the indignity of retracing your steps through the gate and resorting to the Lift and Drag technique. All while parents of well-behaved children pretend not to look.

They overhear what you say and repeat only the bad stuff

Ask them to copy your recitation of the alphabet or the numbers from one to ten, and they become selectively deaf. But accidentally let the swear guard down due to some cockwomble's bad driving and you'll be faced with *"Fuck's sake, man!"* as clear as a bell, for all to hear. Come on in, Social Services.

They lie down on the floor, in public

Usually prompted by the earlier disagreement in the park, this little trick means they always have one up on you because *they don't care what people think.* They will go completely stiff and refuse to stand so you have to pick them up and carry them out of the post office by their coat hood. (Caution: Some coat hoods are detachable. I discovered this when I tried to lift a screaming Henry off the floor outside a charity shop following an apocalyptic tantrum over my unwillingness to buy him a naked Barbie with a wonky fringe.)

They refuse to eat the food you give them

You offer them *one last chance* to start eating it properly before it goes in the bin.

They don't want it.

It goes in the bin.

They do want it.

[Scratches eyes out with discarded bread stick.]

They give away your lazy-parenting secrets

When asked, "What did you do today?" they ignore any of the activities by which you actually tried to be a good parent ("Have a break from CBeebies"), and instead reply, "Watched *Gigglebiz*," "Ate chips!" or "Watched *Gigglebiz*, eating chips!"

They poo at inconvenient times

Regardless of whether they are still in nappies or need your help to use the loo, they save any poo action for other people's houses. Or a supermarket, where there is no customer loo.

They manipulate bribes like a hostage taker

As I've already fessed up, many deals are agreed with my toddler on the sole basis that he will get a biscuit. "Never reward a tantrum," they say. Of course we all agree in *principle*. But after zero sleep, a stressful trip to the shops and a potentially explosive tantrum-bomb on the bus, I have been known to whisper, "Stop whining and you can have a biscuit."

They cry because they are tired

But won't nap. Enough said. (Helpful tip: always remember this is your fault.)

And after all of this, they look so cute when they are sleeping, or when they give you a cuddle, you forgive the bad bits and accept they will be the cause of headaches for the next twenty years.

Tossers they may be, but they are your tossers.

"At my brother's wedding someone at our table said, 'Fuck it!' and our eighteen-month-old decided to repeat it. You can clearly hear us on the wedding video trying to stop him repeating 'Fuck it' by encouraging him to say something else.

"'What does a cow say?'
"'Fuck it!'
"'What does a dog say?'
"'Fuck it!'

"Apparently, the farmyard wasn't very motivated that day."

MARK, WEST SUSSEX

Mum Rage

It's not just the behavior of my children that makes me angry. I think I am angrier *generally* since having kids. My fuse is shorter and I suffer from bouts of seeing red. Chats with other mums both in person and online have led me to conclude that I am not alone.

I usually recognize when I am in the throes of Mum Rage because I find my anger to be ridiculously disproportionate to the actual situation. The following are common causes:

Abuse of "Parent and Child" parking spaces

We've all seen some badass rule breaker casually swinging into one of these without a child or with a child aged *sixteen*. Yes, I'm glaring at you as I park in a normal bay. Not because I'm lazy but because, in a standard-width space, it is almost impossible not to scratch the Audi next to me as I heave the car seat out and the toddler exits wielding his lightsaber. Dick.

Short iPad battery life

The iPad, loaded with Angry Birds and/or Lego Juniors, is quite often the only way I can get stuff done. Charging it for a morning is out of the question. The message "5 percent battery remaining" warns me that shit is about to get real. And by "real," I mean my fifteen-minute child-care sabbatical to clean the loo and change sheets that have been on the bed for a fortnight (six weeks) will be over before it has even started.

Ignorant shoppers

I have a pram. So when you walk at two mph in a gang four friends wide and then stop abruptly outside Urban Outfitters to look at crop tops, I will ram it into your ankles.

Other people's children

Mainly at the park. God, *the park*. If my own child doesn't share the play equipment, or he shouts, whines and makes incessant screeching noises, it's pretty annoying. When this behavior is demonstrated by a child who doesn't belong to me, it's intolerable. I often find myself glaring angrily over the climbing frame at somebody else's child with a look that says, "My son wants a turn. Stop hogging the slide by climbing up it. I don't care that you are two." (Although I follow this with a Nod of Sympathy to the parent.)

Husbands

Loo roll left balanced on the empty loo-roll holder. Sock balls (that have fallen out of the bottom of jeans) left on the bedroom floor. Empty cereal boxes and juice cartons left on the side for the recycling-box fairy. No.

Lack of consideration from child-free friends

Yes, I should still be able to function like a normal member of society. Yes, I'd still love to see you. But when you text me to ask if I fancy meeting in town in *half an hour* I can do nothing but a kind of combined laugh/cry where a bit of wee comes out. Half an hour? Jesus, with me having the kids in tow, you're lucky if I can get ready in half a *day*.

Opinions from strangers

This is actually not something I have ever got massively wound up about, but I have witnessed many angry mums spitting responses to those unhelpful pearls of wisdom offered by people unknown to them. ("I know it *sounds* like she's hungry, but she's just been fed, actually," and, "Yes, somebody is a bit cross. That's why she's *screaming*.") It's always an old person, too. Comedy gold.

Yummy Mummies

Actually, this isn't Mum Rage at all. It's jealousy, pure and simple. I'm jealous of mums who have the time, money and inclination for pedicures, eyebrow threading and a personal trainer. Mums who are never seen sporting yesterday's outfit or deciding they can "get away with" another day of dry shampoo. Mums who have purchased trendy clothes they have somehow managed to *try on*. Mums whose houses have interior-design schemes and seasonal home accessories. (Scatter cushions, you say? I have those: my children are always scattering our cushions.) Jealousy is ugly, I know. Haters gonna hate, and I'm a hater. I must shake it off. I am adding this to next year's resolutions (which I won't keep . . .).

The Sugarcoating of
Social Media

SOCIAL MEDIA is a lie.

Bullshit, bullshit, bullshit.

The end.

Just kidding. I'd best not leave it there (particularly as social media is the lifeblood of my blog, the blog which, incidentally, landed me this here book gig). I must stress, therefore, that there is a lot I *love* about social media and, sad as it may sound, I probably couldn't function professionally without it. If I ever meet Mark Zuckerberg I'll snog his face off.

The beef I have with social media is less about the social-media channels themselves and more about how we, as parents, choose to use social media. What we choose to *share*.

I spent the best part of two years wondering how everybody else made parenting look so easy, how they managed to look so happy all the time, how their *kids* were so happy all the time. What the hell was their secret? Gradually, with corroboration from an in-box bursting with messages from other parents, it dawned on me that my assessment of how well everybody else was coping (and how poorly I was coping in comparison) was more often than not rooted in what I had seen on social media.

This was a mistake on my part, but it turns out it's an easy mistake to make, particularly when you are tired, feel vulnerable and are convinced that your children are broken because, despite buying vibrating bouncers and bathing them in relaxing lavender bubbles, they won't bloody sleep.

The trouble with Facebook and the like is that, if you are anything like me, the friends you are connected to are not all people you genuinely class as "friends" in the true sense of the word. I'm not saying they are people you don't like, just that they are people you don't really know very well (or don't know very well *anymore*): people you went to school with, colleagues from work, second cousins twice removed and some random girl you did sambuca shots with at somebody's hen do in Torquay.

I love a good Facebook stalk. I've been known to waste hours perusing the homes and maternity outfits of schoolfriends who were always trendier than me (slightly embarrassing if people I am Facebook-friends-but-not-really-proper-friends with read this book and now know I've been through all three albums of their holiday snaps). Whatever, the reality is that I still don't really *know* them. I may know what car they drive and what their kids are called; I may know how much weight they lost at Slimming World and what their lodge looked like at Center Parcs. Occasionally, I might find I know too much about the "cheating wanker" of an ex-boyfriend who messed them around. But if I know nothing about them beyond what they choose to share on Facebook, then I cannot really claim to know them at all.

I cannot claim to know how they're truly coping with the breakup from that cheating wanker, I cannot claim to know if they are happy in the life choices they have made and I certainly cannot claim to know how they are coping with parenthood. With my rational head on, I know all of this, yet on the days I feel like I am failing at motherhood those feelings are only exacerbated by glancing at a summary of my friends' timelines, all of which are full to bursting with happiness, and at their Instagram feeds, where there is so much *smiling* and so much #momentcherishing. I have even found myself making assessments of the overall well-being and happiness of mums I have never met but have followed from afar via their tweets and blogs.

If you were to believe social media, every other bugger is enjoying parenthood but you. Those beautiful shots of kids on beaches, snuggly selfies on sofas, posh meals out, loved-up mummy and daddy smiles (#forever) and general family bliss quite rightly deserve a like and a comment. They are the good bits and it is only natural we would want to share them.

We hit delete on the photos that give us four chins. We crop the snaps where our children look anything other than cute. Generally, we feel compelled to share the statuses that reflect good news, good friends and good times. And these good times are made all the more amazing by that Valencia filter on Instagram. (I swear, that filter's magic. I actually quite like myself when I'm shrouded in the Valencia glow, and that's saying something, because I've wanted a nose job all my life.)

When friends have babies, we wait in anticipation for those adorable first hospital pics where the baby lies in one of those wheely plastic cribs with a strategically placed bunny comforter. Weeks later, we might be treated to a sleepy postfeed-cuddle snap or a close-up of tiny hands or feet, all the stuff that makes our ovaries holler that they are ready to do it again. (Mine are proper hollering since having Jude, and my brain just has to keep telling them to pipe the hell down.) What we cannot presume to know is what has happened before those pictures, between those pictures, behind those pictures. Most of the stuff that happens day in, day out just isn't really share-worthy.

What isn't shared is the everyday trials and tribulations of normal life. The humdrum. For every day my boys have spent walking on the beach wrapped up snug and sporting rosy cheeks and impish grins, we have spent ten days at home completing our usual toys, coloring, TV, snack, park, more TV, more snacks daily circuit. For every nice shot I own of them sitting looking cherubic, I have at least ten more that will never see the light of day on my timeline. For every "this little monkey got me up early" status there will be another "well, this is shit, I'm unbearably knackered" post somewhere along the line. Five days after having Jude, I shared a picture of me and the boys out on a family walk and enjoyed seeing the "Wow, you look really well!" comments trickle in. It was a much-needed boost. I *did* look well, because I had run the straightener through the front third of my hair, put makeup on in the car and pinched my cheeks to look healthier than I felt. The reality of my life five days postbirth, however, was spending 90 percent of the day breastfeeding in my dressing gown, sporting a greasy bun and a face pale from moderate iron deficiency.

I'm sure it's the same for us all—our instinct is to share the airbrushed version, the Instagram edit, those specially selected statuses. The unedited photos, the mundane everyday posts and the days we would sell a kidney to have one bastard teatime where *nobody is crying* are the real news feeds and go unreported.

I have sensed a shift in this, though, I think. With the increase in parent bloggers and forums, and communities like my Facebook page (where mums freely post the not-so-glossy bits), I think we are starting to see a bit more of a balance. And wouldn't it be boring to see *just* the crappier bits? I follow mums on Instagram whose kids are always immaculately turned out in stylish clobber, whose nails are never peeling at the sides like mine are and whose houses have kitchens with islands and pastel food mixers which feature in their baking vlogs. I bloody love their Instalives. It's pure escapism and I admire the sheer beauty of those pictures. I only joke about their perfect-parent Yummy Mummy lives because I'm jealous (there, I've admitted it twice now; *I'm jealous*—one for luck).

As a new mum, I found myself fed up with blogs filled with messy-play ideas alongside pictures of trendy children holding hands in sunny meadows (#creatingmemories). But thousands of people *do* want to see this stuff and are equally bored (and offended, as I've been told a few times, whoops) by pictures of children having tantrums and swear-filled rants from parents driven to despair (#passthewine). Some bloggers, including many I have admired from afar, will probably never blog about the shittier side of life at home with kids and, by the same token, I'd rather not blog about the charming (but uneventful) family walk we had on Dartmoor at the weekend and the essential picnic-basket items I packed. I doubt I could add much value to your day if I did, not least because none of us would be in trendy clothes, I am shit at taking pictures and a packet of rice cakes plus lemon squash is about my picnic limit. My point here is that you need to take *everything* you see and read by other parents online—those you know and those you have never met—with a pinch of salt.

So this is just a cautionary tale. We'll probably all continue using Instagram (God bless you, Valencia), we'll periodically pose our kids for portraits and post happy-birthday messages to our babies when they turn one (even though they can't read). We just need to remember that social media is a selective snapshot and is never the full story. It's not always the most helpful place to look when you are having a shitty day. Instead I tend to WhatsApp friends with messages like "Kill. Me. Now," as I find more comfort in their responses than I do in a virtual wall of super-happy times.

It was probably a bit harsh of me to assert that social media is a lie. "Lie" is too strong. "Selectively edited account of reality" sounds fairer. I'll continue to greatly enjoy perusing other people's selectively edited accounts of reality, of course—I just need to remember that pinch of salt.

"When friends look at my holiday photos on Facebook and say, 'It looks like you had a nice time!' I can only reply with, 'Yeah, it does, doesn't it?' Funnily enough, I don't snap pictures of my husband having a half-hour strop because he left the picnic bag somewhere and this became my fault somehow, or the children kicking seven shades of shit out of each other."

LAURA, SOUTHEAST LONDON

Having Kids: The Best and Worst Bits

Noting the tendency for us parents to selectively edit what we post, I've come up with the following summary of what life with kids is like. I do hope it's a balanced assessment . . . Let's get the worst bits over with first.

The Worst Bits

The noise
Crying, whining, screaming, shouting, "Mummy, Mummy, Mummy, *Mummy*?" At times relentless, this symphony of vocal demands drills into your skull and makes you throw a baking tray across the kitchen in an act of anger release (possibly; just something I've heard). Add an array of noisy

toys to the mix and you'll find yourself texting your other half with one clear instruction: pick up some wine.

Always being late

It doesn't matter what time you get up, how long you have to get ready or how organized you have been in packing a bag the night before, it is almost impossible to get out of the house on time. Just as we are about to leave, we encounter Henry's daily poo (fifteen minutes while he reads the Smyths toy catalog; yes, really), declarations of sudden and unbearable hunger (but no, neither child would like an apple) and shouts of "Where the fuck is his fucking coat?" After all of this, we are almost always behind schedule, I am almost always sweating and there is almost always something I've neglected to pack. (I refuse to go back unless this forgotten item is baby wipes, nappies or one of the children.)

Pre-kids, I was an impressively punctual lunch date. I'm now one of those annoying people who say, "Sorry. I'm running really late," and/or, "Oh dear . . . was that today?"

"'Shoes on.' Such a simple instruction and yet one that ages me at least ten years, daily."
JOANNE, GLOUCESTER

Mealtimes

I could devote a whole book to the perils of mealtimes. I've noticed that most sensible families wait until the kids are in bed before they attempt to make their own tea (well, supper, as I suspect they don't eat until eight p.m.). Maybe we are a strange minority, but we all eat together at around six p.m. (bang smack in the middle of the witching hour, I know), and we all eat the same thing. I'd be bloody starving by eight o'clock, plus, that's practically my bedtime; how do people wait so long?

Anyway, dining with a baby and a three-year-old is more often than not total carnage. Apparently, it will get better, so I am sticking with it. Until such a time, I will continue to shovel rice into my gob while picking up the finger-food buffet that Jude has thrown on the floor in its entirety and bribing Henry to eat his vegetables ("If you eat all your green beans, you can have a biscuit").

Lack of sleep

An obvious one, I know, but isn't sleep precious? A full night's sleep is like a magic sprightliness potion that we all take for granted until we are forced to go cold turkey on the maternity ward. (This was not aided by the woman in the bed next to me who kept waking an already fractious Henry by *shouting*, "Oh, no, my baby. Don't cry, my baby," at her own baby, who I can only presume is now deaf.)

I can recall month after month of exhaustedly fannying around on eBay during Henry's three a.m. feed; it felt like I never *wasn't* awake at three a.m. One time, a bundle of secondhand baby clothes turned up at our house and I had no recollection of bidding on it. I had done so in a delirious state. If sleep were a drug, I would be the first to lock myself in the bathroom and snort it.

Children's TV

Where do I start?! Although it is a lifeline in all manner of situations, you will adopt a love/hate relationship with kids' TV. Love because it buys you half an hour to tidy up (check Facebook). Hate because some of it is truly insufferable. Like *Bubble Guppies*. Holy mother of Bubble Gupping God, that program is irritating. And one day you will, worryingly, realize that you have seen every episode of *Peppa Pig* at least five times, that you are engaging in online discussions about the unrealistically impeccable behavior of *Topsy and Tim* (aka Twatsy and Tim) and that you have formed theories about the residents of Pontypandy. (Could Norman Price be Fireman Sam's secret love child? There's no sign of Mr. Price, Sam is *always* far too forgiving about the fact that Norman's a total arsehole and they are both ginger. Definite grounds for a DNA test.) Don't even get me started on *In the Night Garden*. What the actual fuck is that all about?

Kids are disgusting

I mean, they *are*. Not all the time, of course. Sometimes kids are lovely, but a significant proportion of your life will be spent wiping bums, picking boogies off your clothing and sniffing trouser crotches to see if they are clean (your children's trousers, I mean; you should not be doing this for an adult partner). Potty-training Henry went well on paper (he no longer wears a nappy and instead uses a loo—high fives all round), but nothing could have prepared me for the first time I was faced with a fully formed human turd in a plastic pot. Granted, that was where it was *meant* to go, where I had encouraged Henry to deposit it, but never before had I displayed an external reaction so at odds with every sense in my body. "Such a clever boy! Well done, my darling!" I beamed, while retching on my way to drop this longed-for potty deposit down the loo (cue more retching, the immediate requirement of a loo brush and bleach and having to open every downstairs window).

Pictures and stories I've been sent over the last year have opened my eyes to new levels of disgustingness: poo smeared on walls, baby sick caught unwillingly in the mouths of parents, toddlers secretly snacking on dog food, babies eating their own snot off the floor . . . I'll stop there.

Shopping

I don't know why I self-inflict the trauma of going shopping with my kids. I'm not talking about the supermarket big shop here (also hell with kids, but kind of essential). I'm talking about clothes shopping. *Shopping* shopping. Going "uptown." I know how it plays out. I bloody *know*, and yet still I embark on these ventures.

Recently, a trip to town began with me displaying an embarrassingly low level of authority over a hyperactive Henry in M&S. As usual, I started speaking in my very measured middle-class-mum voice . . . "We don't run off, Henry darling; come here, please" . . . and ended up shrieking in my *Jeremy Kyle*–mum voice, *"For God's sake, come back here!* Right, no time on the iPad today, and you can forget about Christmas!" (Yep, continuing to make those threats I'll never uphold.) The entire trip was dictated by who needed a bottle and who needed the loo, and I gave up all hope of trying to nip into any of *my* shops. You simply do not *nip* anywhere with small children. Shopping online is where it's at.

Being ill

When you've got kids, you can't pull a sickie even when you are genuinely sick. You will have to feed, dress and entertain small people who will make your headache worse and ask you why your eyes look puffy. The handful of days so far when I have been proper poorly and James has been unable to take a day off have been pretty dark. They always serve as a brutal reminder that your own needs really aren't as important anymore. (You can forget sulking about that, though. There are lunches to be made and superhero battles to act out.)

Nothing is sacred

Literally, *nothing.* I have no issue with my boys seeing me naked. I have no issue with them seeing me go to the loo. I have no issue with them seeing me buy tampons. But sometimes, just *sometimes,* it would be nice to shave my legs, have a wee or consider menstruation-product options in peace (they are a taxable luxury item, after all). These days, I count an unaccompanied trip to the loo as "me time." I suspect I am not alone in this, but it still strikes me as a slightly sorry state of affairs.

"While in Waitrose, trying to act posh, my three-year-old boy said very loudly (as I picked up some tampons), 'Yes, you need more string up your bum, don't you?'"

ANONYMOUS, WINDSOR

It's certainly not all a sorry state, though . . .

The Best Bits

They love you unconditionally

The power of a cuddle or a smile cannot be underestimated. Those little arms around your neck, a little face snuggled into your chest, a simple declaration of "I love you, Mummy" or the unbeatable sight of a grin and outstretched arms is enough to make your heart melt. (It's even more of a result when it's not immediately followed by "Now can I have a biscuit?") There are times when the boys hurt themselves or are unsure of something and only a cuddle from me or James will do. They want Mum or Dad, they *need* Mum or

Dad, and, despite this being in many ways unsurprising (we live with them; we are their constants), I still feel incredibly honored. Those outward displays of the family bond are really very special, and at times they are enough to transform a what's-the-bloody-point? day into an aren't-we-lucky? day.

The laughter

Admittedly, I am very quick to comment on how discouraging life with kids can be, but the biggest flip side to all that is the laughter. Living with kids is hilarious, not just because they are happy to dance around naked and do impressions of Chewbacca but because they say the most ridiculous things. I couldn't breathe for laughing the day the British Gas man came to service the boiler and Henry assessed him, with confident certainty, to be "a man—not got a fanny." (I've since gathered that most parents use words like "foo" or "twinkle" as vagina alternatives rather than the more widely used "fanny," but I hadn't realized this so told Henry that it was willies and fannies.)

He regularly asks me if I can read him the KFC. He means Roald Dahl's *The BFG*, but, shamefully, KFC must be at the forefront of his mind, thanks to all the nights I've given up on cooking and sent James out for a Bargain Bucket. When *Big Hero 6* came out at the cinema he remarked that he would quite like a "Big Hero sex toy." Sniggers all round. Sometimes we put some music on and watch both our boys parading naked around the kitchen, with zero inhibitions and dance moves so hysterical they have me in tears. Our house is filled with laughter every day and, in spite of their prebedtime arsiness, my boys can light up a room with their giggles. Laughter has saved me on many a tough day.

"My three-year-old calls fish fingers 'shitmingers' (it took us ages to stop laughing at that one—actually, no . . . we still crack up) and flapjack is 'crapjack.' We don't eat out."
HEIDI, NORWICH

Christmas

I always loved Christmas as a child, but as I got older, I think it lost some of its sparkle. It became more about the work Christmas party and having a few days off to gorge on turkey and Quality Streets than it did about the family traditions of Christmas Day.

That sparkle is reignited when you have children. The very thought of decorating the tree, wrapping presents and the boys discovering that Father Christmas has been is enough to give me goose bumps. Christmas serves as a reminder that all the turbulence of the preceding year has been worth it. Another thing is that we are very relaxed about what the kids eat on Christmas Day, so we don't fall out, even at the dinner table (which is just as well, as Henry shouted, "*Yuk!* Take it away!" at the Christmas-dinner offering of 2013).

Holidays

I'll be honest, holidays probably straddle the best and worst bits of having kids, because a trip anywhere with small children, in the UK or abroad, is *not* the relaxing all-inclusive beach vacation of yesteryear. My very wise best friend once described taking kids on holiday as "the same shit, different location." In many ways, that's a fair assessment.

However, there is something quite remarkable about being on holiday. Maybe it's escaping the same four walls, or the fact that you find yourself removed from the mountains of things to do at home—whatever it is, I always feel more relaxed and better able to enjoy the boys on holiday, tantrums and all. Watching Jude toddle around on Crantock Beach in Cornwall last summer, absolutely delighted at having the freedom to explore, while James and Henry made sand castles and I closed my eyes for just the briefest of moments to drink in the sunshine, was such a happy moment. It was one of those moments I wish I could have bottled: another moment when it all came good.

The future

Ultimately, that's what it's all about, isn't it? On the darkest of sleep-deprived days, when I can't sigh without one of the boys interrupting, when I throw out the skinniest of skinny jeans because they are no longer realistic, when I wonder if we will ever be able to afford a holiday again, I think ahead to five years' time, ten years' time, twenty years, even, when my babies will be causing havoc at school, or bringing girls home as teenagers, or having babies of their own. All the times to come when I will be so very thankful that two became four and we created the most important recipe for happiness: a family. *We are a family.*

That's the best bit of all.

Part Five

CUT YOURSELF SOME SLACK

"Wobbles don't make you
a bad parent."

An Open Letter to the Mum with the Red Coat

Dear Mum with the Red Coat,

You probably won't remember me.

I saw you at the park on a rainy afternoon last week. I felt inclined to keep looking over and smiling at you because I sensed you were having a shit day. Actually, I more than sensed it . . . you looked bloody miserable. Your kids were kicking off and you had a "when did this become my life?" face on. I recognized the face because I wear it interchangeably with my "somebody make it stop" face.

It was for this reason that I made a passing "Nightmare, aren't they?" comment, to which you responded with a very small smile.

You were probably distracted by your toddler (who had taken off both shoes, lobbed them from the climbing frame and was refusing to come down) and also by your baby, who—for the love of God!—you couldn't get to stop crying. Of course, you might just have chosen not to engage in conversation with me because you heard my son declare, "Farty knickers bum-bum head" in close proximity to all the other children (he does that a lot).

But I had a sneaky suspicion you were in actual fact more troubled by the behavior of your *own* children. Your face was red, and you looked kind of sheepish.

I just wanted to say something.

I wanted to let you know that you really didn't need to feel embarrassed that day. Granted, your children were being total shits. I mean, they *were*. But that isn't a reflection on your parenting and it isn't a reflection on you. By all means, rage at them, swear under your breath, cry, get the emergency snacks out as bribery—hell, do whatever you need to. But please don't check over your shoulder as if you are anticipating a judgmental glare.

We are in this together.

I get it. I do. When my eldest develops tactical jelly legs and I resort to dragging his deadweight out of the play area and across half a football pitch, it is difficult *not* to clock the stares. And when your son shouted, "I'm not coming down! I hate you!" it was really quite loud—so, naturally, people had a gander.

But you then also felt the need to whisper (at a volume much louder than a true whisper), "It's not time for your milkies yet, sweetheart, you've just been fed," which, though directed at your screaming baby, appeared very much to be for our benefit (me and the other parent bystanders, I mean). As if you were worried we would think, "She really should feed her baby."

We didn't think that.

I'm sure you had already fed her, winded her and tried to soothe her, like anyone would, singing softly about the little fishies on the little dishies and the fucking boats coming in. She just wasn't having any of it.

We have all been there.

Jeez Louise, I'm no parenting expert, but I'm pretty confident in my assertion that sometimes kids are simply shitty. All day.

It's true that I never read this exact piece of advice in any of the Gina Ford or Jo Frost parenting manuals, but I imagine it's in there as a footnote somewhere, or at least it should be. ("If you can't get the child to do any of this shit, it's probably because today is his total-knobhead day," or similar.)

You are doing your best in an impossible job, and that afternoon was particularly impossible for you. Get angry about it, laugh about it (I'm sorry, but his dramatic shout of *"I want a new mum!"* across the roundabout was hilarious) and then draw a line under it.

Trip to the park—failed. So what?

File it in the Absolute Bloody Disaster drawer and start again. There's a Tesco Express within sight of that roundabout where you can grab a bottle of grown-up grape juice (and further snack bribes) on the way home.

Stick your fingers up and say, "Screw you, rainy Wednesday!" Tomorrow is a new day. Of course, the kids might be shitty again tomorrow. But they might not.

Because here's the thing. *Somebody's* children have to be the worst behaved in the park. They just do. The law of averages suggests that sometimes those kids will belong to you.

So the next time another mum pipes up with an "Urgh, kids are a bloody nightmare, aren't they?" comment, please know that she is not slagging you off, or your children. She is just offering you the space to have a moan. She gets it. Because she, too, owns a teething baby and a toddler who likes to "play dead" on the pavement.

Lovely coat, by the way.

Best wishes,
The Unmumsy Mum, forever living in
hope that other mums will return
the understanding Nod of Sympathy

I wrote this in March 2015 and have no idea whether Red Coat Mum ever read it. I like to think she did. Mainly, I'm just pleased to have heard from so many parents who have subsequently messaged to say, "I've had a red-coat day today." We all have those days. I wear mine so often I could moonlight at Butlin's.

Just One of Those Days

BEFORE I BECAME a parent I rarely considered the "type" of parent I would be, but I was certain of one thing: I would not be a shouty one. I was quite sure that my future self would never be found screeching at my children in the street.

I turned my nose up at the mum I saw yelling in the supermarket. How very undignified. How *common*. I tutted at the mother on the bus who snapped at her offspring for their unruly behavior. I think a smack was involved and the whispered threat of a "thick ear." It was all a bit unseemly. I used to feel sad when I heard uninspiring and abrupt answers to questions from curious children whose parents were clearly too lazy to offer any explanation over and above "Because I said so." Shame on them.

Silently, I was forming opinions about their parenting;

judging them from afar. I couldn't foresee a time when I would ever lose my rag in that way. Hardly a good example to set for the kids, is it? Scoff scoff.

It will come as no great surprise, therefore, that karma came and kicked me in the arse. After three years of small-child wrestling, my rag gets lost a lot. I have become *that* mother the pre-mum me would have tutted at. Not all of the time; I like to think there are times when I keep my cool. But I have been at the heart of yelling-in-the-street behavior that would see me fit right in on Jeremy Kyle's show, having a chat with Graham about anger management (and no doubt taking a lie-detector test that would have James storming onto the stage and throwing a chair at Security—seriously, why do people on *that show* take a lie-detector test when *they know they have lied*? How stupid do you have to be? I digress).

Anyway, it has since dawned on me that my judgment of angry parents stemmed from my complete ignorance about the context of *what had come before*. I had witnessed the boiling point but not observed the hours of simmering that preceded it. My on-the-spot appraisals of the situation were deeply unfair.

So I'm sincerely really sorry, Supermarket Mum. When I saw you totally lose it with your little girl in the Co-op I dismissed you as another awful parent and felt sad for your child. It never occurred to me to consider the events that had unfolded before you reached the Co-op. I'll never know exactly what went down that morning, but, with the benefit of hindsight (and having bred two supermarket-aisle escapees of my own), I can now hazard a pretty good guess.

It's likely your little girl had refused to put her shoes on, still fuming from the earlier cereal drama (where you had given her Cheerios because she had asked for Cheerios, but when you presented her with a bowl of Cheerios she suddenly remembered she hated Cheerios).

It's likely your little girl had screamed so loudly you had missed the postman knocking at the door with a parcel, the parcel you had waited in for the entire day before. The parcel that no doubt contained toys or clothes for your Cheerio-refusing child and absolutely nothing new for yourself, because the only interesting catalog deliveries you sign for are for next door.

It's likely she had arched her back as you attempted to strap her into the car and, midrestraint, had kicked you in the face.

It's likely she definitely didn't need a wee as she left the house but definitely did need one two minutes later, when you were stuck at the traffic lights.

It's likely she had been demanding snack bribes to make her sit nicely in the supermarket trolley and, after exhausting the last of the raisin boxes, you allowed her to get down on the proviso she stay close to you at all times—an instruction she immediately ignored as she bolted for the checkouts . . .

So, while making a break for freedom from the tinned-foods aisle really wasn't the biggest deal in itself, I now understand why it might have been the final straw. You weren't overreacting; you had simply hit your limit. I'm sure you know as well as I do that yelling, *"I've had enough of you today! Come back here! Your birthday is canceled!"* never really helps the situation, but, sometimes, it's involuntary. It just comes out.

I'm sorry, Bus Mum. Because, all things considered, there wasn't a lot you could do on that bus. Your kids were, quite frankly, a humiliation, and shouting and/or restraining them was just about the only way you could show the other passengers (me included) that you didn't think their antisocial behavior was okay either. I really don't know what I would have done differently. I've always harped on about my love for boundaries and discipline, but, at times, I have zero control over my children. It really pains me to admit that, but it's true.

I'm sorry to all the "Because I said so" parents I have scorned. The day you said, "Hmmm," and "Yes, dear," and "Be quiet," in response to intelligent questions from your children, I had not witnessed the *million and one* other questions that had come before, like:

"Why is it Wednesday?"

"Can I have a treat later? What time is later? When can I have a treat? Is it later yet?"

"What is cereal? What is cereal? But what is it? Can I have some cereal? Nooooo, not Cheerios!"

I get it now. Because I've been there.

One time when I was shopping in Lidl, Henry kicked off so badly I shouted at him and we both stood crying in the Random Aisle. (If you've never ventured to Lidl, the Random Aisle houses surprising goods like snorkels and knickers and men's walking boots and is usually smack bang in the middle of the shop, which is in itself both peculiar and intriguing. I once bought a tent-peg mallet, and we don't even have a tent.)

Another time, we had nothing in the house for lunch so I "nipped" (yeah, right) to the supermarket to get some food and, after persistent screaming (and staring), abandoned the basket and headed straight home again without having bought anything. I cooked us rice and peas with a side helping of cheese cubes because the thought of another public outing was too much.

The ever-curious Henry once grilled me for an hour about Floyd, the family cat, who had just been put down. I spent a full hour explaining that Floyd had not been well, that he would go to "the Rainbow"—not ideal, but I was put on the spot and was avoiding the introduction of heaven (see also "For You, Mum," page 244). I explained gently that Floyd was not coming back because he had gone to sleep forever. That nobody lives forever, but we can still remember the loved ones we've lost every day. We had even taken Henry to the vet's with us to have the deed done and, after snotty tears of despair from me (I was pregnant with Jude at the time, and I swear the cat thought I was putting him down to make room for the baby), I really thought I'd done a good job at explaining the circle of life . . .

And then Henry piped up with, "When is Floyd coming back, Mummy?"

For fuck's sake—we'd left the vet's without the cat and had spent an hour talking about death. It didn't get much more final.

"He isn't," I told him with a sigh.

"Why not?"

"Because he isn't," was all I had left in my locker.

These days, I live in hope of earning redemption for my pre-parent judginess by dishing out Nods of Sympathy whenever I witness these situations. I no longer take part in the strangers' "control your child" tutting chorus of shame. I smile and nod quite pointedly in the hope it sends the message "We've all been there. He's being unreasonable. I have your back."

RIP Floyd the Cat (2003–2014)

"A recent shoe-shop experience with my two-year-old culminated in her screaming, 'My mummy's hurting me!!' over and over again to the horrified shoppers (I had put a sock on her foot). I then had to buy some flashing shoes that cost more than my own shoes (which don't even flash, FFS) just to get the hell out of there before someone called Social Services."
LYDIA, TWICKENHAM

F**k You, Supermum

IN THE MONTHS after Jude was born I found myself feeling frazzled and short-tempered. In fact, I spent at least two thirds of autumn/winter 2014 sitting in my dressing gown watching *Paw Patrol* and eating Bourbons. I'd lost my mojo.

I've really never been one for New Year's resolutions, apart from the time when I vowed to stop sucking my thumb. Despite a warning from Mum and Dad that I'd end up with Bugs Bunny teeth, it has remained a failed resolution of mine for twenty-nine years. (True story—I'm almost thirty, and I still suck my thumb.) Anyway, quite uncharacteristically, I woke up on New Year's Day 2015 feeling full of promise.

Perhaps I was feeling virtuous due to my complete lack of hangover (this was less out of choice and more out of an obligation not to contaminate my breast milk with Prosecco). Perhaps because the New Year marks a new start, it just felt like 2015 marked *our* new start as a completed family of four. I was leaving pregnancy, childbirth and stubborn placentas behind me and cracking on with life as a mum of two. This was it!

Whatever it was, when spring came onto the horizon and the end of maternity leave (and my return to work) loomed in sight, I vowed that I would make some all-important changes to my parenting behavior. I would do so much more with the kids. I would make the most of it—2015 would *not* be a repeat of the Bourbon-eating Nickelodeon marathons.

My parenting resolutions (as mentally committed to on 1 January 2015) were as follows:

- The children would watch less TV.
- I would spend less than 75 percent of the day on my iPhone.
- Biscuits would *not* be used as bribes. In fact, biscuits wouldn't really be needed *at all*, because I'd make lunchtimes healthy and fun by creating animal faces with quinoa and blueberries.
- There would be an abundance of long walks in wellies.
- There would be cake baking.
- There would be finger painting and puzzle solving and fort building.

Two thousand fifteen would be the year of the Supermum.

"So how did it go?" I hear you ask, though I'm guessing, deep down, you know the answer. That if Supermum really had rocked up with her quinoa animal faces, I would be writing an altogether different book. It would be called something like "How to Be Supermum" and it would have a cover bearing a picture of a smiling mother and children in Daz-white T-shirts doing some sort of craft activity (without Mum cursing the "bastard glitter").

So, no, it didn't go that well.

And, as I have since seen in *another* New Year, I can officially provide a progress report for *all* the months subsequent to New Year 2015—these were, after all, resolutions designed to extend beyond one year toward forever Supermumdom. So here goes.

- The children do not watch less TV. Sometimes I fear we are watching even more TV as I enlist child care in the form of both *Mister Maker* and *Mr. Bloom* in the same day and later head off to bed with the theme to bloody *Bubble Guppies* in my head.
- I still check my phone an unacceptable number of times throughout the day. It's compulsive. If we go out for the day at the weekend, I *have* started leaving my phone at home or switched off in the glove box of the car. When I am on my own with the boys, though, I'm often on the cusp of developing Repetitive Strain Injury from excessive social-media refreshing. Sometimes, I pretend I need the loo so I can check on the headlines (like what Buzz-Feed has to say about Kim and Kanye).
- Biscuits are still used as bribes. Daily (hourly). Henry's bribes have also been upgraded to doughnuts and *CBeebies* magazines. *I know, I know.* Awful parenting tactic. But it works, and I'm bloody knackered and weak willed (and now drowning in freebie plastic magazine tat).

- We haven't been on loads of long walks. Maybe four or five (three). But we have worn wellies! And one time Henry brought back some sticks from the forest, which he pretended were hunting harpoons, so he's practically Bear Grylls now.

- I've voluntarily entered into just one cake-baking episode, and I was wound up after five minutes because Henry's exclusive contribution was to eat the sweets earmarked for decorating it and hover precariously close to the hot oven while I sweated about third-degree burns.

- I have, at least, purchased some paints and halfheartedly started a "craft box," but I'd be lying if I said we've *enjoyed* this crafty time. I had this image in my mind of us creating Pinterest-worthy paintings, but all Henry wants to do is mix *all* the colors on the same piece of paper to create a soppy, wet, brown pile of shite. Don't even talk to me about puzzles or glitter or twatty sequins.

So I've failed, right?

Well, yes, I have failed. In fact, this wannabe Supermum fell flat on her arse within a matter of hours and has continued to chaotically bum-shuffle her way through parenting ever since.

Yet I am totally at peace with this failure, and I'll tell you why.

"Supermum" is an arse. She is an entirely fabricated patchwork of Cath Kidston dresses, superfood smoothies, 4x4 school-run vehicles and Mary Berry cookbooks. Supermum can be found on the Joules website sporting skinny jeans, a casual gilet and styled-to-look-messy hair, or hanging out in the kitchen of her uncluttered and stylish barn conversion, which smells like fruitcake.

Supermum bathes in a magic patience elixir and never gets cross. Her children never protest-plank in the post office or shout their mouths off about farts and bums because she has enforced *boundaries*. She has two children (one of each, obviously) and they never watch telly unless it is a snow day, when they drink hot chocolate under a tartan blanket because she is so much fucking fun.

Despite having spent many months of parenthood being jealous of Supermum, I've come to realize it's a bit like being jealous of Barbie and her unattainable hip/waist/bust ratio. Supermum can take a flying fuck at a rolling chia-seed muffin for all I care because *Supermum is not real*.

Nobody manages to be Supermum all of the time.

There are days when I have a bloody good stab at it. One time, we went for a walk in the woods, built a fort in the living room, did some finger painting and made hot chocolate all in the same day (yes, I Instagrammed those things and felt quite smug). But it's a bit like Supermum role-play: the everyday run-of-the-mill reality is something altogether different.

I'd love to take my kids on an adventure every day. And bake some gingerbread. And make Tracy Island out of washing-up bottles. But, on an average weekday, Henry charges around at a hundred mph, shouting, "I am Buzz Lightyear!" and I have to battle with four loads of washing because some nappies do *not* do their job and Jude has been sick and the home-insurance renewal needs posting and stuff needs sterilizing and I need a shower because three days' worth of dry shampoo has created an unsightly white buildup . . . On these days, I actually can't be arsed to go on a sodding adventure or facilitate messy play in a house which already looks like Hurricane Rita has struck it.

So I whisk the boys to the park (again) for a quick blast of fresh air and then I come home and put *Mister Maker* on. And give Henry a biscuit. And check Facebook for an hour.

That's life, isn't it? That's just how it is.

Even without the endless crafts, chia seeds and bottomless barrels of patience, my boys seem to think I'm pretty super.

I'm not sure anything else really matters.

"I was totally knackered and overwhelmed with the lifestyle change. It wasn't rosy like everyone has you believe and I remember just wanting to scream, 'Piss off!' at the other mums at playgroup who were discussing how to make glitter Play-Doh."
STEPH, LINCOLN

Mum Guilt

I HATE FEELING GUILTY.

Since becoming a parent I have experienced guilt at a level over and above the guilt I'd encountered before. Over and above the guilt experienced when telling my friend my phone had died when I couldn't be arsed to chat, or after drunkenly saying something I didn't mean (or maybe did mean but shouldn't have said), or after eating a More to Share bag of Maltesers (without sharing) and not doing any exercise.

This newfound guilt is harder to shake off. It sits there churning in the gut, churning around the heart—sometimes, it feels like an overall churn of the whole torso region.

I've discovered I am not alone in this guilt overload.

Since starting the blog, I have been inundated with messages from mums that are rooted in feelings of guilt and inadequacy, messages containing phrases like "I just feel so bad about X" and "I wish I could be more like Y." And I usually reply: "You really shouldn't beat yourself up about X or Y; motherhood is bloody hard work! You're doing your best and the fact you're questioning how you're doing shows you care. You're never alone; stick with it, my dear, xx."

And I then feel like the fakest of fake hypocrites because *I* spend my days beating myself up and rarely find comfort in the fact that I'm "doing my best." My best just isn't good enough. So, really, I suppose I should also be feeling guilty for telling people there's no need to feel guilty when I still feel guilty. So. Much. Guilt.

Last year, when deliberating on writing a blog post about Mum Guilt, I thought it might be helpful to write down all the things I have felt guilty about since becoming a parent. So here's my Guilt List, which has evolved over the years:

- I didn't take folic acid for the first seven weeks of my pregnancy because I didn't know I was pregnant.
- I should have bought the premium pregnancy vitamins and not the budget ones.
- I didn't take it easy at work in the third trimester; I worked flat-out and probably damaged baby Henry.
- I should have had a drug-free birth. I drugged my baby.
- I wish I had managed to breastfeed for longer. I haven't protected Henry from diseases.
- I shouldn't have got angry when he cried all the time as a baby. Nobody else shouts at a crying baby.

- I went back to work early and left him. What kind of mother does that out of *choice*?
- I don't do enough with him when I'm at home. He's bored.
- *I'm* bored when I'm at home. How awful is that?
- I shout too much. I'm too impatient.
- I'm in some way "cheating" on Henry by having another baby. He will no longer be my Whole World.
- I mostly forgot to take *any* vitamins during pregnancy two.
- I also had the odd glass of wine and the recommendation is: no alcohol. I may only have had a unit here or a unit there, but if there's something wrong with my baby everybody will know it is my fault.
- I wished for a girl, and that's why Jude's birth was so awful. I deserved it.
- I haven't taken Jude to any baby classes. Henry did baby massage and music groups in his first year. Jude is neglected.
- I spend far too much time checking my phone.
- I don't cook enough healthy stuff. We eat too much convenience food.
- I let Henry have too many snacks. His teeth are going to fall out.
- We don't have a nice garden. I've ruined my boys' childhood because we live in an urban jungle.
- I've bought shoes not meticulously fitted in Clarks, which will no doubt lead to foot deformities.
- I left Henry crying at preschool, and he knows now that I am just a great big *liar* because I said I'd never leave him.

- I often wish the time from five p.m. until bedtime would just die. Some days, I wish this from as early as eleven a.m. I'm not appreciating my time with them.
- I'm not a Fun Mum. I don't do much craft/baking/painting. I'm boring and shit.

Reading my list again once I'd written it was pretty staggering. Some of it is so ridiculous it would be hilarious if it wasn't just a bit bloody sad.

I wonder if hindsight irons out the guilt. I'm no longer sweating about the missed folic acid, the drugs in labor and the shorter than recommended time spent breastfeeding—it is what it is. I also know (with the backup testimonies of friends and family) that Henry really did cry all the time. I was at my wits' end with the crying and, while I'm not proud of the day I shouted, *"What the fucking hell is wrong with you?"* (while crying myself), I know I spent far more of his first year cuddling him and singing to him. The guilt from those early days has lifted.

But I'm still living some of the list. The pang that I should be doing more exciting stuff with the boys, that I should be playing with them more, that I should be living in the moment and enjoying them, that I should stop looking at my watch to see how much more is left of the afternoon and then tweeting about my disbelief at how much more is left of the afternoon.

In a few years' time I have no doubt the guilt will evolve into a new form. Not being able to do the school run every day due to work commitments, not spending enough time encouraging them to do their homework, not having the money for swish holidays abroad.

In fact, I think I'm already suffering from *future* guilt in anticipation of the day my boys are old enough to read this book. Guilt in anticipation of their exposure to my warts-and-all account of motherhood. Maybe I'll wish I had let them think I'd enjoyed every second and never once pined for the life I had before they arrived.

But in the game of Guilt Top Trumps, I'm keeping those guilt-fueled messages from other mums in my mind and pushing thoughts of potential future guilt to the back of it.

So what is to be done about this perpetual guilt train we find ourselves on? I can't very well tell you to "give yourself a break" and "stop beating yourself up" when I'm often failing to heed my own advice. So my appeal is a simple one.

Share the guilt.

Not share the *actual* guilt, but share your feelings of guilt. With other people. With other parents. Because you can bet your bottom dollar that guilt is all around and after half an hour of discussing who has the most reason to be guilty, you'll probably just conclude you're all a bunch of unnecessarily guilty numpties and start feeling guilty for wasting too much time feeling guilty.

I'm still standing by my assertion that, if nothing else, feeling guilty shows you care.

Genuinely, though, there's no need to feel guilty about most of the crap on my list. Half a glass of Pinot Grigio and some forgotten vitamins in pregnancy do not make you a saboteur of the baby vessel. An epidural does not line your child up for meth addiction. It probably is good to put the phone down and play with the kids more, but don't get distressed about "not doing enough." I like to think that time together is enough.

Plus, they can do all that crafty shit at playgroup. Guilt only becomes regret if you let a toddler loose with sequins.

"I couldn't understand why I wasn't basking in the glow of new motherhood that everyone else talks about. Every day felt like a struggle. I felt tremendous guilt about that. My daughter is hilarious and, in retrospect, it all seems worth it."

SARA, CARDIFF

You Don't Have to Explain Yourself to Anyone

MUMS ARE DEFENSIVE creatures.

We feel the need to explain *why* we do things. Why we feel things. Why we behave in certain ways. To explain that this isn't *usually* what we'd do but we were short of time/it's a treat/ we are having a difficult day . . .

There are times when I find the urge to justify my parenting choices pretty overwhelming. When I hear myself adding a rationale to my every move, as if I'm anticipating the "How come you do it like that, then?" question. More often than not, that question is never asked, but I can't seem to stop myself throwing an explanation out there anyway, just in case. I've developed an involuntary habit where I add a line of defense to all my responses concerning the way I do things with the boys.

I'm pretty sure my aforementioned Mum Guilt is behind

this. The underlying doubt (I might not be doing the right thing; I might not be good enough) creeps in and manifests itself in a slightly self-protective tone. At the heart of it all, I think I'm just frightened other parents will think I'm a crap mum.

It's definitely not just me. I hear other mums explaining themselves all the time.

And I've come to the conclusion that this is completely unnecessary. There is just no need. The following are genuine justifications I've been offered during everyday playgroup/park conversations with other mums and the responses I *wish* I'd given (I think I probably just nodded):

"I only got him a pacifier because he whines a lot and it helps him settle. I don't really agree with them . . ."

Relax. A pacifier is clearly working for you. I wish our two had taken a pacifier, but, alas, they did not. There was no pacifying my babies, more's the pity.

"She wouldn't usually have a chocolate biscuit as her midmorning snack, but we're running low on fruit . . ."

Chill out. Honestly. So she's having a biscuit. I can see she's happy and healthy and I'm sure she has her fair share of healthy snacks, too. But she likes chocolate biscuits because she's a child; I've yet to meet a child who *doesn't* like chocolate biscuits. You promised her one if she used the loo at playgroup. It's all good. Zero justification needed.

"The TV's only on because I need to get some washing done and it provides a distraction for half an hour; it wouldn't usually be on . . ."

There's nothing wrong with a bit of TV. I know wall-to-wall cartoons are never ideal, but, let's face it, we all need to get stuff done, right? Thank God for *CBeebies*, the child minder who is never on holiday.

I have noticed that chats about breastfeeding also promote these defensive outpourings. And I do understand that: breastfeeding is a very emotive topic. I have experienced firsthand the temptation to tell the world/his wife/his dog about my decision to switch to bottle feeding when my baby was four months. One time, I started outlining Henry's reflux issues and slow weight gain to the woman behind me in Boots. She neither needed nor wanted to hear Henry's pediatric referral history, but she was gifted our entire feeding story anyway. I think it was more for my benefit than for hers—I was feeling hormonal and delicate and just a little bit paranoid that I was being judged for having a tub of formula in my basket. I felt an impulse to make it known that *I had tried.*

But I know that when *I* ask a new mum in general conversation, "How's the feeding going?" and she is *not* breastfeeding, I'm genuinely not digging for an explanation. It is just a question that helps establish what to talk about; I'm not going to start ranting about leaky breast pads if she hasn't ever breastfed and, by the same token, I'm not going to ask her if she'd recommend Aptamil Hungry milk if she's exclusively breastfeeding. I'm just asking how it's going. There is no requirement for her to elaborate on all the problems the baby had latching on, on his low birth weight or the mastitis that prompted the decision to switch to formula. Of course, if she wants to chat about all of those things, I'm all ears. But she actually *needs* to say no more.

Perhaps we feel inclined to continue saying more because, as parents, we fear being judged. We're worried that we will be assessed and found sadly lacking. Maybe, sometimes, we hope our explanations will nip that judgment in the bud: "If I just explain why I'm doing it this way she won't think badly of me . . ."

The truth is, she still might. Because here's the thing: some people will judge you anyway.

I have met mums who definitely *are* judging you. And me. And every other parent. A small handful of mums who think they are doing everything right. In fact, they *know* they are doing it right because they've bought all the parenting manuals and read every consumer report dating back to the first infant-travel system ever invented. It's their way or the highway. These are the mums who come out with uninvited tips that start with "I have always found . . ." or "I'd be careful doing that with her because I've read . . ."

When I first had Henry I would nod and smile at unsolicited advice from those mums and then head home to further wallow in my failings as a mother, feeling embarrassed at having been outed as an unprofessional parent. But, second time around, I developed the ability to ignore unwanted intervention.* And now, when

---

*Please don't think I'm confusing helpful recommendations with unwelcome opinions. Sometimes, the safety or well-being of a child is at the heart of advice given, and if somebody wants to question how my car seat is fitted or point out a choking hazard, I'm all ears. Sometimes, other parents will see you struggling and think, I've been there and I can help. It's only the preachy "You really should do it this way" brigade

well-meaning but immensely interfering mums offer nuggets of wisdom such as "You know, you really shouldn't use the word 'naughty' because it is so negative and might affect his behavioral development" (yes, really: actual quote right there), I shoot a small but firmly dismissive smile which I hope says, "When I need your advice, I'll ask for it. Until such a time, you can piss off."

So if you're reading this and you have been on the receiving end of Mrs. Judgy Knickers's pearls of wisdom, I urge you to take no notice. You don't need to justify your every parenting move, and, more to the point, doing so to prevent being judged by other mums is a fruitless exercise—there will always be a small handful who think they know best. Disregard the risk of being judged and hold your head up high.

Because, actually, I think *not* justifying your every move comes across quite well. An "I do this because it suits me and my family" attitude commands respect. It indicates a confidence in one's own ability to decide what is *right*. Not right in the preachy-preachy, holier-than-thou, total authority in the history of everything that was ever right *right*, but right for you. For your kids. For your family.

"No, I don't breastfeed."

"Yes, she's three and still in nappies."

"I'm not going back to work at all, actually."

Enough said.

You really don't have to justify yourself to anyone. Explain your decisions only if you want to. One-size parenting can never

---

who I am giving the middle finger to. Most mums are absolute gems. Solidarity to the parent pack.

fit all; we're all different and, heaven knows, our kids are all different—you'll never please all of the people all of the time.

For me, perhaps the sharpest observation of the day-to-day dealings we have with the differing beliefs of other parents came when a dad who had been reading all the comments on my blog messaged me simply to say: "Opinions are like arseholes. Everybody has one."

If that doesn't make you smile the next time you meet a Mrs. Judgy Knickers, I don't know what will.

"When we were on holiday, the kids were tired and cranky all day and there was nowhere to put the eight-month-old who couldn't yet crawl but would happily face-plant off the sofa. I ended up telling the family we had got our dates mixed up regarding coming home, when really we were coming home a day early because, quite frankly, it was a bit shit."

KASIE, THE WIRRAL

It's Okay to Lose Your Shit

It is well documented that I lose my shit on a regular basis.*

So much so that I now get daily messages via my blog page from fellow shit losers—whose solidarity is much appreciated, particularly when I find myself once again sitting in the downstairs loo talking myself down from collapsing in the living room and banging my head on the floor repeatedly (this often seems tempting).

Shit-losing triggers I have documented on my blog have included:

---

*I recognize that "losing my shit" is an urban expression and I'm really *not* very urban, but I overheard and imitated it a few years ago and it has stuck. As has "shit just got real." Shit gets real a lot.

- A screaming Henry tantrum about his shoelaces (they weren't the right shoelaces, even though they were the shoelaces that came with the shoes).
- The fourth sleepsuit change in as many hours due to Jude's feces tornado.
- General narkiness from the pair of them over a prolonged period, followed by kicking and smacking (by them, not me).
- An assortment of other testing life-at-home moments, like when the washing machine blew up just after Henry wet the bed.

Most days, my feelings of despair can be fixed with a bit of a moan and a nice cup of tea. I once saw a sign that read "A cup of tea solves everything," and I concur that there aren't many things in life that can't be made at least a touch better by a cup of tea or the promise of something stronger when the kids are in bed.

"Roll on, bedtime, and the G&T with my name on it!" I've chuckled, because it's all rather rib tickling.

But some days it's not funny at all.

Some days, I don't feel the urge to poke my eyes out, or shout, or drink G&T from a tin (though I am partial to G&T in a tin, and every so often it's three for two in our local shop).

Some days, I don't feel the urge to take myself for a time-out in the downstairs loo.

Some days, I don't feel the urge to do any of these things because some days, I actually feel quite *desperate*. Days when my children have pushed me to my absolute limit and I truly don't know what to do.

I know I plod through most weeks just fine, and that, pretty much, I'm just jesting when I assert that I'm "not cut out for motherhood." But there are days when I genuinely worry that this is true: when I carry around a really big knot in my tummy, a knot which, on the odd occasion, has put me off my food and left me feeling sad, a knot that cannot be fixed with a cup of tea.

Sometimes, even if only momentarily, I can't shake off the feeling that I am a big, fat failure of motherhood.

When I'm losing my temper at the whining in the car, or lying to Henry that the slide is still wet because I can't face another tedious trip to the park, or wishing the week away because three more days of only me and them seems like a lifetime . . . I panic that there's something wrong with me.

Why don't I enjoy being at home?

Why do I find it so damn hard?

Do other mums feel like this?

Do other mums struggle?

Do other mums find the simultaneous baby-and-toddler crying so draining that they get in the shower and join in? So *everyone* is crying in the bathroom at the same time? (God knows what my neighbors must think.)

In those moments of doubt, a dark cloud descends, pushes down on my shoulders and I panic: *I'm so crap at being a parent. I can't do it.* I torture myself further by measuring my maternal prowess against mums in parenting magazines and mums on Instagram who #livelaughlove. I always fail when I compare myself with those mums and their perma-smiles and their Fun Mum activities and their impressively fashionable outfits. *Why aren't they wearing yesterday's hoodie?* And then, just as quickly as the cloud descended, it starts to lift (the break in the cloud often coinciding with James's return from work and/or the *CBeebies* bedtime song) and I snap myself out of it. And I think, *What a bloody stupid measuring stick, you bloody stupid woman.* Because, deep down, I know that the crying in the bathroom and the white lies about the weather and the wanting to kill someone in the car . . . well, I know those things are not ideal, but I also know that they are not a true indication of my Mum Score.

The one and only measurement I need is my boys. How they're doing. How they're feeling. Because, above all else, and more important to me than anything else, I want them always to know that they are loved.

One night, after a particularly tough day just a few months after Jude was born, I genuinely hit a wall of despair. I stopped joking about "not being cut out for this shit" and told James I was failing. Hands down, without the need for any independent adjudication, I was *the* shittest mother in the history of shit mothers.

I had spent the day wishing I were somewhere else.

I didn't deserve them.

They deserved better than me.

And then bedtime arrived and Jude fell asleep midfeed and I sat with him for ten minutes in the semidark, stroking his little ears. And he smiled. It might have been wind because ten minutes later he was sick in my bra, but, regardless of whether it was a windy smile or a proper smile, he looked as contented as any baby on a Gina Ford book cover. And then I popped in to say good night to Henry and, instead of tucking him in, I got under the covers and read him two stories. And marveled at how much he understood, at how smart and funny and *happy* he is.

"Love you to the moon and back, nighty nighty pajama pajama," I told him, chuckling to myself on the way out as he replied, "Nighty nighty pajama pajama knickers on your head" (he was very much in an underwear-on-head stage), and I sank onto the sofa to watch *I'm a Celebrity* with this happy, instinctive feeling that I was doing all right. We were all right.

Maybe it's okay to have days when you're not fine.

When you're not coping.

When you want to divorce your children because they have self-activated "arsehole" mode again.

Wobbly days.

Admittedly, some of my wobbles are a darn sight wobblier than I'd like, and if I could eliminate all wobbliness, I would. But I can't. And, looking at my boys, I don't think I need to.

So if, like me, you have been torturing yourself for having shit-losing wobbles, I just want to say something.

Wobbles don't make you a bad parent.

They make you a *real person*.

Wobble away, my friends.

You are doing just fine.

WE ALL HAVE testing days, when everything gets a bit much—that's just par for the motherhood course, I think.

However, if you are feeling like you can't cope (and it's more than just a shitty day), please don't think you have to struggle alone. Speak to your GP and, for further resources, see page 273.

"I have often sat and cried because, in that moment, I did not even like my own child, and what kind of mum doesn't like their own child?"

GINA, BRISTOL

Spinning Plates

I CAN'T REMEMBER the last time I didn't have an enormous Things to Do list on the go. Mostly, this list exists in my head and remains in a constant state of flux because I only have room in my confuzzled brain for a certain number of items. I've calculated this number to be around ten, which means "Must get photos of Jude printed because it looks like we only have one son" always drops off the list to make room for "Phone the bank" and "Buy Grandad's birthday card." When something becomes particularly urgent, it is transferred to the sophisticated diary I purchased from Paperchase back when I still held out hope of becoming an organized mother. The reminders within usually start as prompts scribbled in ballpoint pen ("Book Henry's injections"; "E-mail outstanding invoices"), but when I still have not honored them two weeks later, they are underlined, highlighted and eventually circled angrily *with* the highlighter until the overkeen, urgent highlighting bleeds through to next week's page. The once-classy diary is now a mess of highlighted incompetence.

The ongoing Things to Do list in my *head* would be even messier if you could see it; it's a chaotic amalgamation of stuff I actually *need* to do and things I *should* be doing (and am therefore worrying about not doing):

Buy a bath mat, sort out visits to prospective primary schools (other parents have done this already!), take bags of clothes to charity shop (check the loft: more clothes to go?), finish writing next batch of chapters, bleach and bicarb the shower sealant to remove mold spots, buy bin bags, send thank-you cards for presents (too late?—send text apologizing for usual crap tardiness), plan more meals with vegetables before the kids get scurvy, reply to whatshername about the thingamajig, read to Jude or at very least sign him up for a class because he has not been to any classes, get Henry some new trousers, write magazine column, order replacement sink, do some proper exercise and/or weights for bingo wings, see doctor about CON-TRACEPTION (this cannot happen again), redesign shambles of a blog page, get quote for fixing dodgy windows downstairs, check upcoming birthday-party dates (have I double-booked again?), investigate cracked phone screen repair, start using hand cream on crinkly hands, organize the night out I've canceled three times already, living room is a dump—sort out toy storage (IKEA?), phone my sister.

I'm forever plate spinning: darting around underneath massive plates on flimsy sticks, trying my best to keep the Motherhood plate spinning smoothly with my left hand while leaning over to spin the precariously balancing Career plate with my right. I simply cannot afford to let either of them fall, but sometimes my arms are just so tired. With all my efforts invested in the double Motherhood and Career spin, I have no choice but to let the Household plate (on which sit the insurance renewals, the boiler service, the housework and all the crap that comes with being an adult) come tumbling off its stick. Praise be to James, who calmly catches the most urgent of this plate's contents as it falls by, paying off the required credit-card amount and reading the meters. I don't even know where the meters are (true story).

I've always been really house-proud ("a place for everything and everything in its place"), but—and it really pains me to say this—my standards have slipped. These days, it's more "a place for nothing and nothing in its place." Our once-organized cupboards are now filled to bursting with crap (literally, bursting; most days, I have to kick the contents to get the doors to shut). There is dust absolutely everywhere you can't see and in most of the places you can see. The once smear-free glass TV stand (glass was a bad move, I know that now) is constantly smudged with tiny fingerprints. Every now and again, when I'm attempting to unwind in front of *Location, Location, Location*, I find my eyes drawn to a mouth-shaped smear on the television screen which unmistakably tells me that Jude has (again) been trying to kiss those weird *Waybuloo* creatures straight after eating his porridge.

The Household plate has not been the only casualty. Once, there was also a Me-Time Plate, piled generously high with things like having my highlights done, reading those trashy magazines about celeb mums who are a size zero three hours after giving birth, swimming half a mile and seeing friends for long-overdue catch-ups. This plate is no longer spinning at all, but its loss of momentum was gradual, so it fell without smashing and now sits sadly on the floor, waiting for the one time of year when my roots get so bad that I simply *have* to act, or the biannual occurrence of my actually going for a beauty treatment. I did, in fact, have the first treatment in a course of HD brow sessions (so I would look like Cara Delevingne, obviously), but I never got around to booking any more sessions and bought an eyebrow pencil for a fiver instead.

The truth is, if I ever do find the time to finish painting the kitchen units (the ones I started painting eighteen months ago), vacuum *behind* the TV stand (not blitzed since the Great Pregnancy Nesting of 2014) or fake-tan more than half of my body, I will no doubt feel guilty about not investing that time in the competing and equally overflowing plates of Motherhood and Career.

I always pictured myself as a career mum. I pictured skirt suits, boardrooms and rushing from the delivery of an epic presentation to my girls' (yep) nativity plays, leaving fellow nativity-goers impressed with my desire and ability to *do it all*. When I went off on maternity leave the first time, I fully expected to return to my job in finance full-time (or, at the very least, four days a week), slotting straight back into the career I had worked so very hard to establish. I held this belief for a few months of that first maternity stint before I became consumed with a deep-rooted wobble that I would never match up to my pre-mum working self. I wanted to return to that job—really I did—but I was so frightened about no longer being able to give it everything. When I looked at Henry's little face and felt the way he clung to me whenever I left the room, I began to feel a churn in my tummy about leaving him for the best part of each week and missing bath time and story time every day. I'm well aware that it wouldn't have been *impossible*—many women (including mums I know) have returned to similar positions, and I have nothing but respect for them (and maybe just a smidgen of jealousy).

Yet I felt—and I suspect I am not alone—that *something* had to give. I had become accustomed to working late and logging on at weekends because I was so desperate to impress. The pre-parent Work Me was twenty-four years old with a company car, nice blouses and heels. She thrived on the drama of trying to get a finance proposal completed before returning home to a bottle of wine and further checking of her BlackBerry. The pre-parent me was a bit of a martyr, if I'm honest ("I'll reply to this work e-mail at ten p.m. because I'm *so* busy and it'll show everyone how dedicated I am"), but it suited me at the time because, other than rearranging our already tidy cupboards and going out for power walks while listening to my iPod (both hobbies of mine at the time), I didn't really have anything else to *do* during the week. Even when I was ill I found myself working from home in bed. I was 100 percent committed to my job.

The Working-Mum Me, whose waist-to-breast ratio now looks decidedly disappointing in those same blouses, who can't escape the house on time without vomit crust on her tights, who has a five p.m. teatime routine to get back for and often has to cancel meetings at the last minute due to child-care issues, is not capable of being 100 percent committed to any job.

I cried when I handed in my notice in favor of a part-time position with fewer targets at the local university. I felt like I was giving up on my career, but, to this day, I know that I would have been frustrated if I'd carried on with my earlier career. I would have given it my best shot, but it would have been the best shot possible *as a mum*, the best shot possible between the hours of nine a.m. and five p.m., Monday to Thursday, and not the best shot I had proved myself to be capable of. I simply couldn't bear working alongside the ghost of the ambitious me with the perkier breasts.

I left baby Henry when he was six months old to work at the university, but it was a *part-time* job. Three days a week: the Holy Grail for working mothers. Part-time work, I was told, would give me the *best of both worlds*. I think that was what I needed to hear: that I could have it all, that I could do it all, that I could *be* it all. I have changed jobs again since then (I'm currently doing the writing thing—for a while, anyway; we'll see how it goes), but I still work part-time, because I've settled into the three-day rhythm with the boys.

Which means I still have it all, right? The best of both worlds? Well, I don't really know is my honest answer. In many ways, I still think part-time work is the most favorable option for our family—I get a couple of weekdays at home to enjoy motherhood and a few days at work to be something other than their primary caregiver (as I've said already, I admire women who are full-time mums, but I could never cope with it).

I like the balance, I really do, but there are days when I wonder if having the best of both worlds is an unreachable ambition. I know there are many jobs nowadays where mums and dads can work flexibly, or work from home, but there are many more where there is no option of getting back for bedtimes, no possibility of altering working patterns, and I have seen *so* many mums take a step back from their pursuit of promotion to honor their heartfelt instinct that they should spend some time at home, too.

There are days when I lose my concentration with the dual plate spinning and I feel massively discouraged by my inability to excel at either role. I wish I could take on more in the work context, but I can't. I wish I could answer all my e-mails and chat to important people on the phone without having to wipe Henry's bum midconversation, but I can't. I wish I could go to some of the snazzy work events in London I've been invited to, but I can't. In the same way, I still feel guilty when I pass my children over to somebody else three days out of five, when James and I both get in too late from work to cook anything other than fish fingers, when at bedtime on a Wednesday Henry asks me if I can take him to the park tomorrow and I reply, "Not tomorrow, sweetheart, Mummy's working," and then he asks if I can take him the day after tomorrow and I reply, "Mummy's working then, too, but I'll take you soon, I promise."

So, no, I don't always think I have the *best* of both worlds—I don't do either the work thing or the mum thing at full capacity, but I can't imagine giving either up and concentrating exclusively on the other. I'm managing a *bit* of both worlds, and maybe that is the best one can hope for. Perhaps my plummeting levels of organization and household cleanliness are the realistic fallout from a desire to have it all. Supermum would manage it all, of course she would, but for the rest of us something really does have to give.

My family comes first—it always will—and work comes a very close second, because work helps me feel more like myself and slightly less batshit crazy. All the other stuff—all the everyday organizational items whirring around my brain—well, that's all bound to suffer in the process, and I think I need to accept that (or maybe get a cleaner, though I fear I would feel tempted to clean up before the cleaner arrived, such is the state of the shower-scum buildup).

There are only so many hours in the day, right?

It is probably for this reason that I found myself waiting four days to receive the PIN reminder for a debit card I swore blind they "never bloody sent me any PIN for!" but which I had in fact received weeks before and written down somewhere safe.

It is probably for this reason that Sunday afternoon has become the only day I am guaranteed to attempt to cook a meal where the vegetables don't come out of a tin.

It is probably for this reason that Fred, my best friend's little boy, will probably continue to receive a birthday present from me in December when I send a bumper Christmas parcel to "combine the two" (his birthday is in July).

It is probably for this reason that I find the never-ending piles of toy crap bloody irritating but still kick them under the sofa to "worry about tomorrow."

As parents, we already have too much on our plate. Our brains are constantly ticking over with stuff: stuff we should be doing, stuff we ought to do more of, stuff we've forgotten to do, stuff we'd love to do if we had the time . . . Maybe all we can do is decide which plates we absolutely have to keep in motion—the plates that make us happy, the plates that have become core to our being—and learn to breathe deeply as the contents of the other plates are sacrificed.

You can't do it all.

Though I really do need to buy a bath mat.

For You, Mum

I'm writing a book, Mum. An actual book! I'm so bloody chuffed about that, and yet I feel heartbroken as I write this chapter. I'm heartbroken that you will never get to read it. Perhaps I'm stupid for writing it, but there are things in my head that I want to say, and if I don't get them down in this book, I'm not sure what will become of them. I don't want them to remain unwritten, even though I know they will remain unread by the person who really matters. Oh, how I wish that you *could* read them.

On a recent trip into town, I spied a woman of about my age walking out of Gap, and I have never been more jealous of a stranger than I was in that moment. She was holding on to something that no amount of money can ever buy me; she was holding on to her mum. They were walking arm in arm, chatting about what they still needed to buy and about possibly going for a coffee first.

It was a strange moment, because part of me wanted to look away, to surround myself with the chaos and buzz of other shoppers and pretend I hadn't seen it. Yet the biggest part of me couldn't tear my eyes away. It was so special and beautiful that I wanted to shout over to them, to tell them to hold each other tight and savor every minute of every coffee they would have together.

I wish so desperately that you were here. I long to go for coffee with you, and I don't even like coffee. You liked proper coffee on a Sunday with the newspaper; maybe I would have grown to like coffee on a Sunday, too.

I long to link arms and try on clothes together. I long for you to tell me that we should head to M&S first because if I bought something there, I would get "plenty of washes" out of it.

Above all, I long for all the unremarkable and ordinary mother-and-daughter moments we will never have. I wish you could come over to chat about nothing in particular, join me on trips to garden centers and help me with the boys' birthday cakes. I was left unsupervised with Jude's first birthday cake and cocked up the icing. You would never have used the wrong icing. I wish so badly that the boys could have cakes made by their nanny Debbie. People often remark that it's a shame they never got to meet you. It's so much more than a shame. There is a hole in our lives where you should be. Wherever I am, whatever I'm doing, there is something missing. You are missing.

Henry asks about you. He's seen the picture of you on my bedside table, and we've had to explain that, despite you being his nanny, he can't have a sleepover at your house and you will never pick him up to take him swimming. I told him that you had gone to "the Rainbow" and when he asked me, "Does she like it there?" it took every ounce of my being not to sob.

I don't believe in "the Rainbow," or heaven, or life after death. Deep down, I know that when somebody dies, that is it. We keep their memory alive by talking about them, but, physically and spiritually, they have gone. In many ways, it would be lovely to believe that you are somewhere watching over me—so many kind people have told me that you are, in an attempt to offer comfort, I suspect, but I don't believe it for a second. I just don't.

Before Henry asked where his nanny had gone, I had thought I would tell him straight; but, when it came to it, my pre-planned "people don't actually go anywhere when they die, darling" came out as "Nanny Debbie has gone to the Rainbow with Floyd the Cat and all the other people who were too poorly to stay on planet Earth."

Someday soon, I will have to explain to him that when I say we are going to Nanny Debbie's beach, we are actually going to the beautiful spot where we scattered your ashes.

It is all so remarkably sad.

Sometimes, I sit and worry about how you must have felt during those last few months you were in hospital. I was too young to worry at the time—I had schoolwork to do, and when visiting time was over, Dad would take us home for tea. Now when I think about you sitting alone, it makes me want to go back and spend every minute of those hospital hours with you. You wanted us to carry on as normal, to study hard. At the time, keeping busy was the right thing to do, but all too soon you were gone, and we couldn't sit with you anymore.

I'd give anything to have that time again, to sit with you, hold your hand and never leave your side. I was so worried about you leaving us that I never really considered how worried *you* must have been, how desperate you must have felt, knowing that we would grow up without you. I now understand the feelings a mum has for her children, and the thought of leaving Henry and Jude to grow up without me is simply unbearable. It must have been so hard for you.

Being a mum is so hard. You made it look easy, even though you were undergoing treatment for so many years. You were a mumsy mum. You had patience, you cooked us nice things and could sew badges onto jumpers and, despite your teaching full-time, I never felt that you weren't there (bar the odd school-assembly performance when you actually *weren't* there, but, all things considered, I'm prepared to let that go). You were—and still are—my parenting idol. You are the closest thing I've ever known to a real Supermum, and I'm so proud that the real Supermum was *my mum*.

Now I'm a mum. I'm a mum who's shit at baking and shit at sewing, who loses her cool over things she just can't seem to develop patience for. I often think I could be a better mum if I had you here to help me; that being a mum without a mum is just so bloody unfair.

I try to remember I'm not without a mum, that you are here with me every day. Not physically here with me, not looking over me or guiding me from your VIP spot on a mythical rainbow, but with me here in my head and in my heart, wrapped in all those memories I have of such a great childhood. I owe you so much—you gave me a quality of childhood that I am hell-bent on re-creating for your grandsons. You would love them, Mum. They are such wonderful boys. And they would have loved you. Henry would have loved cuddling you. Jude would have loved sitting reading a book with you (in between trying to hit you in the face—it's just a phase, apparently). You would have loved James, too. I chose very wisely there. I have always known you would have given him the nod.

On days when I struggle the most, when I feel like I am just not cut out for it, when I doubt myself as a mum, well, on those days I keep in mind how brilliant you were. I want to do you proud. I can't promise that my cooking will get better. I can't promise that I won't shout (I'll definitely shout, it just comes out like that). I can't promise that I won't make mistakes and I can't promise that I won't sometimes be slightly less than a great mum.

I can promise you something, though.

I promise I will do my best. You always told me that was what counted, and you were right. I will make sure that my boys are happy and safe and that, above all, they will always know they are loved. I will love them an impossible amount, with all the love in my heart and extra love on your behalf.

I will give them the extra cuddles you can never give them, and I will tell them that you were the best.

You really were.

I'm so sorry you will never hear me tell them that.

Part Six

WOULDN'T CHANGE IT FOR THE WORLD?

"Some days, I look at my boys and it seems surreal that they are mine."

Before You Know It...

If I'd banked a pound every time I have heard someone say, "They'll grow up too quickly!" I'd have enough money to shop freely in JoJo Maman Bébé. As it is, my refluxy boys have always prided themselves on vomit-staining a new outfit within seconds, and £21 is a lot for a wear-it-once nautical jumper, no? Much safer to go for George at Asda. I digress. "How time flies" is classic parent-to-parent conversation:

"These are the good years; enjoy them."

"One day you'll miss these moments!"

"Before you know it, they'll be at school!"

Generally, I pay little attention to these liberally offered nuggets of parenting wisdom, but I must admit that there were times early on when I found such comments a bit tiresome. The days when Henry refused to move from his chosen protest location (most memorably, the lift in John Lewis, where he had an on-his-belly tantrum which prompted our fellow lift passengers to press the button early and get out). The evenings when I sat amidst crap plastic toys, discarded food flung from the high chair and dirty washing and had no idea where to begin clearing up so instead glanced longingly at the door, imagining the freedom and calm that lay on the other side. The days when Jude screamed for his bottle (the bottle I always seemed to make slightly too hot) or hung off my ankles, smothering my jeans in his miserable teething snot. On those days, I couldn't stop myself concluding that, actually, time wasn't going too quickly *at all*—there was nothing about those moments I could ever possibly miss.

I had never really found myself being emotionally caught up in special occasions and early-years milestones. Not because they weren't special, but because pretty special stuff happens all the time, doesn't it? All around us, every day. So sentimentality over first teeth, unaided rolling-over and suchlike has never really been my thing. I was therefore pretty confident that I would *not* become one of those parents who would dig out the baby photos and say, "Oh, look at him! Just look at how small he was!"

As it turned out, that confidence was misplaced. *I have become that person.*

My first taste of sentimental smushiness hit me in autumn last year as the milestone of Jude's first birthday approached. This state of mind was quite unexpected, not least because I hadn't felt particularly emotional about Henry turning one. (Sorry, H Bomb, we had a cracking day, but I just didn't get teary about it.) Yet the prospect of Jude being one seemed to dance around the periphery of my brain for weeks before the event, popping up when I closed my eyes at night (alongside the repeated daily reminders to book a smear test and take the bottles to the bottle bank).

I found myself wanting to sniff Jude's hair and drink in his babyness. The rational part of me knew that postbirthday, he would be just one day older than he had been the day before; but he would be a *one-year-old*, a walking one-year-old with teeth and those cruiser shoes whose price makes your eyes water when you get to the till. Once they have turned one it's the end of the *proper* baby bit, isn't it? People start referring to their kid's age in years ("He's one, right?"), and I feared I might forever feel tempted to reply, "Well, he's fourteen months/seventeen months/twenty-two months, actually." I mean, how long can that go on for? "Yes, he's 219 months and living in halls at university. Yes, he's well, thanks, still on the fiftieth percentile in the red book, weighing 168 pounds."

James gave me a look of mild amusement mixed with unease when I told him I was sad about Jude turning one. This was uncharted territory: his never-broody wife was demonstrating clear signs of broodiness and, at one point, he did feel it necessary to assert, "Yeah, but we're not having another baby, ever."

Tempting as it would be to wind him up by looking wistfully at baby booties and suggesting hypothetical third-child names, the fact of the matter is I'm pretty certain I don't want another baby. I think that's precisely why I've started to feel a bit delicate—it has dawned on me that I've completed the baby bit. For good. Like a level in a video game.

Level Baby: complete.

In many ways, this is an achievement to high-five. I certainly won't miss the pasta-encrusted high chair, the reflux and the incessant five-to-seven-p.m. whining that makes me want to bash my skull in with the LeapPad. I won't miss the need to cart around multiple bags filled with parenting equipment. I have never been the world's biggest fan of the baby bit, and it would be insincere of me to suggest that I'll miss doing three-hourly feeds or that I will sob over their tiny footprint paintings.

Nevertheless, it is the end of an era. Jude is already looking so grown-up, and experience tells me it won't be long before he starts lobbing lightsabers at my head and asking me to pull his finger. In no time at all, we'll have to potty-train him, introduce him to big-boy pants and go through the whole trouser-wetting rigmarole once more. I did calculate, though, that, by that time, we will have started approximately 1,825 mornings with the changing of a shitty nappy, so even though there will be trouser-wetting incidents to come, I will still be doing a victory dance around the lounge when the final nappy has been disposed of.

Meanwhile, his big brother (now a dab hand at the art of lightsaber lobbing and timely fart execution) has progressed to another level by starting preschool, which has further intensified this sudden rush of nostalgic reflection. Time and again, following testing days at home with Henry, I've muttered, "Roll on, school!" and now I'm not so sure that I meant it. This year, he will start proper school, and the thought of my Henners, my Henry Bear, *my baby* heading into the classroom with his uniform and his book bag already makes my heart hurt. I will no doubt return home from his first school drop-off and cry over baby photos and (sorry in advance to parents of new babies I will meet later this year) it will make me say things like, "Oh, she'll grow up so quickly!" and "Enjoy this time!" because I will selectively have forgotten all about the John Lewis lift incident and find myself craving the days when I could gather both my boys on my lap and sniff their hair without them protesting.

There is so much more to come, of course. More good, more bad and, undoubtedly, more ugly. (I've had hundreds of messages from parents of teenagers telling me that I ain't seen nothing yet, and I can well believe it.) I know I'll have years of school runs and sleepovers and anxiously waiting up before they fall through the door pissed on alcopops, but I also know they will never be as dependent on me as they are in these early years. I'm kind of a big deal to my boys right now and, while clinginess drives me to the point of despair, I'd be lying if I said that it isn't sometimes really *nice* to feel needed. While in many ways, the prospect of their increased independence is quite liberating (hello, weekends away while they stay at Grandad's), in many ways, it is also quite sad.

I'm a bit sad that someday soon, they will both be at school doing hours' worth of stuff I know nothing about. Soon, they will be far too cool to dance with me in the kitchen or creep into my bed for a snuggle.

I will miss those things.

If, right now, you are living with a very small baby who keeps you up half the night/is sick in your bra/showers the Moses basket in yellow feces, or if you have just returned from having to drag a screaming toddler out of Sainsbury's, then it's quite possible you will feel slightly skeptical of my cautionary tale about future nostalgic smushiness. As a first-time mum, I was certainly skeptical of all the mums who told me, "Before you know it, he'll be at school and you'll miss these times!" because school seemed like a *lifetime* away. Yet here I am, selecting primary schools, worrying myself silly that Henry won't cope without his mummy and worrying myself some more that he will undoubtedly cope just fine.

Perhaps sentimentality about the early years is something that cannot be passed on as secondary wisdom. Perhaps you have to discover it for yourself. Perhaps it's simply part and parcel of parenthood that you will have days when you are beyond exasperated at owning small children and then, before you know it, you will wake up and think, I miss their smallness.

I'll stop banging on about how time goes too quickly now and get back to stroking baby photos. You have been warned.

"It's funny, isn't it, how quickly you wish some of the weeks away and then you find yourself wanting those early days back again?"
MHAIRI, NEW MILLS, HIGH PEAK

Does Being a Parent Change Who You Are?

A COUPLE OF WEEKS after Henry was born a friend asked me, "So, do you feel, you know, *different* now you're a mum?"

"No," I said. "Not really."

When I said this, I felt *physically* different. My boobs were like boulders, and half a stone of human had just emerged from my vagina. I'd had finer hours. But, emotionally, mentally, in my head . . . no, I felt very much the same. I looked in the mirror and saw a fatter, more tired version of myself, but it was the Same Old Me.

Holding a baby.

Granted, being a parent had kick-started a massive wave of changes in my life and body, but it wouldn't change my personality, I was certain of that. In spite of the nappies and the muslins and the breast pads, I was just the same.

I had met mums who, to be quite honest, were unrecognizable versions of their pre-mum selves. I don't just mean they had changed physically; I mean they became entirely different people. And I was genuinely quite scared about this happening to me. I was determined not to let the Old Me be swamped by the Mum Me. Motherhood would not change the essence of my being.

Then, recently, I had a bit of a moment in the car. I was alone, on my way to the child minder, and I had the rare chance to put one of *my* CDs on. The first one I pulled out was an old compilation. A mix tape. Among some random '90s R & B and the Killers (my all-time favorite band; love you, Brandon) was Jay-Z's "Niggas in Paris." I know.

At the exact moment I turned up the bit about "muhfuckas" I caught sight of myself in the rearview mirror. I glanced at the Maxi-Cosi car seat and Cat the sun shade. I spied the slightly crinkly corner of my eye and the crap job I had done at concealing my under-eye bags. And, suddenly, I felt like a total twat for singing about muhfuckas. *I felt like a mum.*

The truth was, I'd made that car compilation back in the day, when I was spending hours on the road each week driving to customer appointments in my BMW with its sporty seats and reasonable brake horsepower. Listening to Kanye rap about shit being "cray" in a ten-year-old, sluggish Vauxhall Astra, surrounded by discarded Fruit Shoot bottles and unloved toys (a stray squeaky egg and half a Ninja Turtle) just didn't feel the same. The sun shade, the car seat and the fact I would imminently be swapping Jay-Z for *High School Musical* felt like an obvious marker that my life is no longer the same. I am not the same either.

There are definitely still times when the Same Old Me comes out to play. On a recent night out with old work friends, "I'll stick to gin" went out of the window at seven p.m. Despite three out of five of us being parents, we drunkenly chatted all evening about an array of "normal" things outside the subject of our kids. In fact, there are conversations from that night that I've still not recovered from, including one about a real-life adult sharting-in-bed incident. (If you don't know what sharting is, it's a bit like farting but with messier consequences—I didn't know this risk extended beyond toddlers. I learned a lot that night.)

Even without being rat-arsed, I'm pretty good at chatting about *other* stuff. At playgroup, I'm the first to try to break free from chats about teething and sleep regression and the weight of my baby—not because I'm in any way denying my role as a mother but because, every so often, it would just be nice to chat about *EastEnders*.

I have loads of friends who don't have children. Sometimes, I prefer meeting up with my child-free friends to going on play-dates because hearing about holiday romances, work news and shamelessly trashy gossip from the *Mail* online is a welcome break from discussing child-care vouchers and follow-on milk. Perhaps I live vicariously through the lives of some of my non-parent friends, but I would be lying if I said my life was anything like theirs—and my life not being like theirs has meant I am not entirely like them either. Having children has changed my life, and it has changed me.

It has changed how I think and what is on my mind. I no longer feel carefree. I feel an enormous responsibility not to screw it all up, to make sure I keep my kids safe and happy. I feel anxious that I am not good enough, that they deserve better; because, sometimes, I don't cope all that well. Sometimes, I long for that life when I listened to mix tapes and enjoyed nights out without being expected to go to a birthday party at ten a.m. the next day and pin the tail on the fucking donkey. Party games and noise with a hangover are proper torture territory.

Some days, I look at my boys and it seems surreal that they are mine. Days when I've been masquerading as the Old Me at work and, all of a sudden, it dawns on me that I am responsible for actual proper small human beings and I think, "Shit, how did this happen?" Of course, I *know* how it happened (the stork's delivery was slightly more extreme than I'd imagined), but I still occasionally feel shell-shocked that I am a mum.

I am a mother.

I am a lot more besides, of course. I'm a writer, a blogger (not a cool hipster one, unfortunately), a friend, a wife, a rape helpline volunteer, a remarkably clumsy person with a penchant for gin and iced Chelsea buns who is shit at doing the dishes (apparently, I don't wash them properly—whatever). But if all the aspects of my being were captured in an Excel pie chart, my boys would be the biggest and most significant slice by far (James included, but we won't tell him that).

It is unlikely that anything else in my life will affect me quite as much as having kids has. The impact is colossal. Over and above those silvery stretch marks (did I tell you they are on my *thighs*?) and the logistical impact of keeping two children alive, there is an emotional difference I can't even compute. I challenge anybody to not be affected by that. Being a parent has indeed changed who I am. My boys have changed who I am. But, in many ways, I quite like it.

That shit really is "cray."

"I've definitely reached the point where life as a mother is not quite what I imagined: cheering my son's first potty experience on as he farted in it . . . surely that counts? We were both quite proud."

AMY, ST. ALBANS

"You Don't Know How Lucky You Are"

I CAN'T BRING this book to a close without getting something off my chest. I feel the need to liberate the bee in my bonnet and have a moan. A moan about moaning. A moan about *not* being allowed to moan. (I'm writing this chapter with a glass of wine by my side, because it feels a bit like the sort of chat I'd have with a friend. I would start with a big sigh.)

Occasionally, after having bared my parenting soul through the medium of a blog post, I have found myself under fire for complaining about life with children. For complaining about how having children has made me *feel* and, perhaps, once remarking that if parenting were a paid job I would without hesitation have resigned with immediate effect.

Mostly, bar the odd attack on my use of expletives, these

criticisms have been variations on a "you have no reason to complain" theme:

"You should be more grateful; some people can't have children."

"Why have children at all if you're just going to moan about them?"

"You don't know how lucky you are."

I haven't laughed these comments off or stuck two fingers up to my laptop while muttering, "Oh, piss off, you self-righteous wanker," because I have found myself feeling a bit crushed after reading them. One time, I confided to James that I felt like shutting down the blog (and my social-media pages) and getting on with my life simply as "mum" and not as the Unmumsy Mum, whose parenting attitude was being hung out to dry on the Internet.

Of course, I had no real intention of shutting down the blog so, outwardly, I remained thick-skinned enough to ignore the criticism. A selection of recurring comments were circling my brain, though, niggling away at me and making me feel just a little bit shit. In moments of self-doubt and crisis I usually find that Taylor Swift brings sage advice to the table, but there was a period when I just couldn't heed her "Shake It Off" advice. I think, to a large extent, this was because I knew there was truth in what they were telling me.

I *am* bloody lucky.

I have no reason to complain.

I *should* be more grateful.

I recognize all of these things because I have *perspective*, and perspective is a powerful beast. I have lost count of the number of times I've been having an almighty moan (probably about the kids' incessant whining or my withdrawal symptoms from work or the overall shittiness of a testing day at home) and I've been stopped in my tracks after seeing something, hearing something or reading something that has made me think, "Shit, why am I moaning?"

I've followed stories of parents whose children have disabilities, parents who have lost the love of their life (and parenting partner), parents who have lost children. I've heard stories about couples who have tried for years to become parents and never succeeded, parents who have experienced a beacon of hope by way of IVF only to suffer loss through miscarriage. Just watching the news is often perspective enough; I cried all day after seeing pictures of three-year-old Syrian refugee Alan Kurdi's tiny body washed up on a Turkish beach and vowed never to moan about my life again.

All of these stories are accompanied by completely unimaginable levels of pain and subsequent strength, and they almost always prompt me to have a word with myself about trying to moan less and appreciate more.

I have my boys, our house, my health, *their* health—Christ, I only have to watch one episode of *DIY SOS* and I'm dashing upstairs to hold my babies tight and breathe deep sighs of relief that everything is okay. My lovely mum was only in her forties when she died, and I have grown up knowing that "life is too short." There is a lot to be said for counting one's blessings and recognizing at any given time that it could be so much worse.

(You're sensing a *but* coming, aren't you? You're right, there is one coming.)

I could easily end this chapter with "So count your blessings and stop complaining," but I'm not going to. I'm not going to because I have been mulling over the hundreds of messages I've received from other parents which, cumulatively, have prompted a U-turn in my thoughts.

These parents who message me to tell me they are at their wits' end and struggling to enjoy their day or their week (or, sadly, on occasion, struggling to enjoy parenthood at all) are not people who enjoy moaning. In fact, alongside their honesty about having a difficult time of it, there is almost always an expression of guilt attached to having a moan. They end their messages with "I know I should think myself lucky . . ." or "I know there are people far worse off than me . . ." and while I recognize that I myself have those feelings, I've also started to find them quite frustrating. Mainly, I have the urge to reply, "I *know* you appreciate how lucky you are. *Moaning doesn't mean that you are ungrateful.*" Moaning is part of life. We *should* share our gripes and our worries and our moments of frustration, because doing so helps us all to feel normal.

I think a turning point for me was speaking to a mum who had struggled for ten years to conceive before IVF delivered a miracle daughter. She told me that after a difficult day she had once shouted, "It wasn't fucking worth it!" at a shocked friend before crying tears of guilt for sounding so ungrateful. The fact that her daughter had been such a miracle meant she felt it would simply never be okay to have a moan, despite the fact that, like every other baby, said miracle was sometimes a complete pain in the arse. I knew this mum had perspective, I knew she had thankfulness by the bucketload and, in that moment, I also knew that, however grateful you are, it doesn't make you immune to the odd groan.

I joke about *DIY SOS* and the like, but, genuinely, when I've witnessed the hardships that some of these families have had to face I find myself pledging to think of their heartbreaking situations the next time I feel compelled to start complaining about my trivial concerns.

In reality, this perspective—however impactful—is only ever momentary. Before long I find myself holding a screaming baby while going into battle with a toddler who has refused to put his pants on for the seventy-sixth time. Before long, the madness and frustration of looking after small people gets the better of me and, all of a sudden, without any regard for perspective, I find I've written a blog post jam-packed with whining and sent James a ranty WhatsApp message about being "so fucking fed up" (sorry, James). I just can't seem to hold back the ranting.

Not once have I woken up and thought, I fancy a right good moan today about how much my kids are doing my head in and how it turns out parenting wasn't for me after all. LOL.

That is not how it is.

So I stand shoulder to shoulder with the parents who have sent me ranty messages, and I don't regret my own moany posts, even the one about jacking in the "job," because that was how I felt at the time. I felt angry and frustrated and bored and guilty all rolled into one. Momentarily, I wanted out. Momentarily, I wanted my old life back; the life where I could make it through ten minutes without somebody crying, where I could wee in peace, where I could actually hear the breaking news because the telly wasn't being drowned out by the noise coming from some demonic electronic toy.

In reality, even if handing in my notice *had* been a legitimate option that day, as soon as I had spied the boys' empty beds I would have found myself on my hands and knees begging for my job back. I moan about them not because I am ungrateful but because they drive me to the depths of despair.

Now that I've had more time to digest the critical comments, I've decided that the "Why have kids at all if you're just going to moan about them?" argument is a stupid one. It's a bit like saying, "Well, you chose that job in recruitment, so you can't ever tell me you've had a shitty day because you *chose* to work in recruitment."

Imagine you were offered your dream job: dream position (Tom Hardy's PA), dream firm, dream salary. It is the job you have *chosen*. But rather than working Monday to Friday, eight thirty to five thirty, you work all day every day with no sleep and no unaccompanied loo breaks. You would be forgiven for thinking, "Holy Mother of God, I want a break from this shit" by Wednesday teatime, no? That's parenting. Some days, it's fantastic and I'm so pleased I took the job. Some days, it's hideous and I want my old job back.

Yes, I did decide to have children. I decided this *twice*. I'm never going to hand my children over to somebody else and nor would I want to, but I'm still allowed to say, "Fuck this!" every so often. We all are. Not because we don't appreciate our children or because we are ungrateful for all that is good in our lives but because, sometimes, we will simply feel shitty about a shitty day, and even though our feelings aren't those of loss, trauma or acute anxiety, they are still valid feelings.

Perspective is a wonderful and powerful tool, but it can't always make everything better and it certainly can't improve the witching hour (or two) before bed. I rarely count a crying baby lobbing food from his high chair and a toddler refusing to cooperate on any level as a blessing. There is no obligation to treasure every moment and you should not be made to feel guilty for occasionally opening the griping gates.

This chapter has felt like therapy. I started it feeling slightly scolded by the "You don't know how lucky you are" comments, but I now feel inspired to address all members of the Thou Shalt Not Moan party with one measured and very dignified response.

Dear Thou Shalt Not Moan Enforcers,

Thank you for registering your disapproval of my moaning and for trying to make me feel a bit more shit about my inability to love every second of parenthood.

I have, however, decided to ignore your comments. I don't need you to tell me how lucky I am. I know I am tremendously blessed to have two smashing boys. You might be surprised to find my love for them is actually quite well documented amidst the expletive-heavy rantings.

I am also a human being who feels tested by motherhood and not a robot programmed to remain delighted with life at all times. I do have regard for those less fortunate than myself; I also have regard for the thousands of mums who feel alone when they are having a rotten day. They are not alone, and I intend to keep telling them so.

In short, you can fuck right off.

Warmest regards,

The Unmumsy (but most definitely not Ungrateful) Mum

The Parenting
Roller Coaster

THAT WISE PHILOSOPHER Ronan Keating once told us that life is a roller coaster, and I'm pretty sure he was talking about parenthood.

It's true: I was *fairly* emotionally expressive before having kids. I have been known to shout, "Pick a lane, any lane, you wanker!" while driving. I have also been known to laugh hysterically on drunken nights out and cry at the *Britain's Got Talent* interviews where the contestant explains that it's the first time they've had the courage to sing since their cat died.

I knew there was an emotional range there to start with. But I've *never* known a roller coaster of emotions quite like the last four years of my life and, in many ways, that has proved the hardest adjustment of all.

Gone are the good days and bad days: life is much harder

to classify emotionally now that I'm a mum. Sometimes, I encounter the full spectrum of emotions in one day. Sometimes, I encounter the full spectrum of emotions in one *hour*. It's rarely possible to sense when they will hit.

There are times when I feel angry. Try as I might to suppress those feelings of fury (believe me, I try), there is only so much food refusal, sofa dive-bombing and incessant whining that one mortal can take. I mutter, "For fuck's sake," at least 127 times a day (while sighing) and I hate what the Mum Me sounds like. She sighs too much.

There are times when I feel guilty. For not being the best, for not always *giving* my best and for downgrading overall standards from good to good *enough*. I'm disappointed in my "that'll do" style of parenting, but it turns out "that'll do" is quite often all I've got.

There are times when I feel happy and really bloody thankful, bursting with pride and gratitude for all that I have and all that we are as a family. Those are the times when I find myself laughing at hilarious things the boys have done or smiling until my cheeks hurt, wondering what I could possibly have done to deserve so much greatness in my life.

There are times when I feel scared. Scared of how much I love them. Scared about letting them go out into the big wide world (okay, school, but it is bigger and much wider than the living room). You only have to watch the news at teatime to know there is some seriously messed-up shit going on around us. I feel scared when I can't see them or hear them. Even when they have a sleepover at my mother-in-law's, I can't bear to look at their empty beds because I know it would trick my mind into thinking what if . . . what if the unthinkable ever happened?

And it all takes its toll, doesn't it?

The laughing, then crying, then shouting, then worrying and then laughing some more. It's not surprising parents feel tired. Being a parent is so emotionally draining, so *unpredictable*, that at times I long for calm. I long to go to work and feel mildly stressed about targets before coming home to drink wine without worrying about how I'm doing in my *other* role—the unpaid but more important role, the role that has put me in charge of raising small human beings, the role that has completely and utterly changed my life.

I think back to all the times I have declared, "I would rather be anywhere else!" and, in the heat of those moments, I can assure you that I meant it. Yet I've come to realize that without my boys, *anywhere else* would be empty. Calmer, more predictable, less shouty, with less chance of crying in the downstairs loo, but empty all the same.

Maybe we just have to accept the unpredictability.

To take the crushing lows along with the pretty remarkable highs. To plow through the shower of shit days safe in the knowledge that there are brighter, less shitty days to come.

I think Ronan was right about the roller coaster.

We just gotta ride it.

Resources

The following are some of the organizations that can provide support should you feel unable to cope, or think you might be suffering from postpartum depression.

Postpartum Support International
postpartum.net
1-800-944-4773

The Marcé Society for Perinatal Mental Health
marcesociety.com
615-324-2362

National Institute of Mental Health
nimh.nih.gov

U.S. Department of Health & Human Services
mentalhealth.gov

Acknowledgments

There are so many people I would like to thank, so I will jump straight in. Hannah Ferguson, thank you for believing in this book and for continuing to take such good care of me as my agent. Transworld team, kick-starting the Unmumsy book adventure in the UK: what a remarkably clever and lovely bunch you all are. Thanks to Sarah Levitt for helping me realize my dream of being published stateside and, of course, to Joanna and all the team at Tarcher Perigee for making it happen!

Dad, thank you for *everything* (now is as good a time as any to thank you for the last twenty-nine years). Tina, Becca, Ena, Andrew and all the family who have offered support (particularly with child care, the most useful support of all)—thank you. Thanks to friends and colleagues, old and new, who have helped me to feel excited about taking a leap into the unknown.

Mary-Anne, thank you for all your words of best-friend encouragement and for sharing my blogs far and wide before anybody else did. Mel, thank you for offering a space where I could sigh a lot (and for sometimes joining in with the sighing).

James, my wonderful James, thank you for being levelheaded whenever I "go off on one" and for making me cups of tea even when it's my turn. We make a great team, you and me. Henry and Jude, thank you for inspiring me to write and for making me proud beyond belief. I'm sorry I have at times been too busy typing to notice your shouts of *"Mummy, look at me!"* Let's go on holiday soon, and I'll leave the laptop at home.

Finally, I would like to thank the followers of my blog and social-media pages for reading, sharing and regularly making me cry with laughter at your comments and pictures. You have helped me to feel less like a failing misfit of motherhood and, for that, I am eternally grateful.

If you enjoyed this book, visit

www.tarcherperigee.com

and sign up for TarcherPerigee's e-newsletter to receive special offers, updates on hot new releases, and articles containing the information you need to live the life you want.

tarcherperigee

LEARN. CREATE. GROW.

Connect with the TarcherPerigee Community

· · ·

Stay in touch with favorite authors

Enter giveaway promotions

Read exclusive excerpts

Voice your opinions

Follow us

TarcherPerigee

@TarcherPerigee

@TarcherPerigee

If you would like to place a bulk order of this book, call 1-800-733-3000.